ISAIAH

Chapters 36—66

J. Vernon McGee

THOMAS NELSON PUBLISHERS

Nashville • Atlanta • London • Vancouver

Published in Nashville, Tennessee, by Thomas Nelson, Inc.

Scripture quotations are from the KING JAMES VERSION of the Bible.

Library of Congress Cataloging-in-Publication Data

McGee, J. Vernon (John Vernon), 1904–1988
   [Thru the Bible with J. Vernon McGee]
   Thru the Bible commentary series / J. Vernon McGee.
     p.   cm.
   Reprint. Originally published: Thru the Bible with J. Vernon McGee. 1975.
   Includes bibliographical references.
   ISBN 0-7852-1024-5 (TR)
   ISBN 0-7852-1084-9 (NRM)
   1. Bible—Commentaries. I. Title.
BS491.2.M37   1991
220.7′7—dc20
                          90–41340
                            CIP

Printed in the United States of America

9 — 99

CONTENTS

ISAIAH—CHAPTERS 36—66

PREFACE

The radio broadcasts of the Thru the Bible Radio five-year program were transcribed, edited, and published first in single-volume paperbacks to accommodate the radio audience.

There has been a minimal amount of further editing for this publication. Therefore, these messages are not the word-for-word recording of the taped messages which went out over the air. The changes were necessary to accommodate a reading audience rather than a listening audience.

These are popular messages, prepared originally for a radio audience. They should not be considered a commentary on the entire Bible in any sense of that term. These messages are devoid of any attempt to present a theological or technical commentary on the Bible. Behind these messages is a great deal of research and study in order to interpret the Bible from a popular rather than from a scholarly (and too-often boring) viewpoint.

We have definitely and deliberately attempted "to put the cookies on the bottom shelf so that the kiddies could get them."

The fact that these messages have been translated into many languages for radio broadcasting and have been received with enthusiasm reveals the need for a simple teaching of the whole Bible for the masses of the world.

I am indebted to many people and to many sources for bringing this volume into existence. I should express my especial thanks to my secretary, Gertrude Cutler, who supervised the editorial work; to Dr. Elliott R. Cole, my associate, who handled all the detailed work with the publishers; and finally, to my wife Ruth for tenaciously encouraging me from the beginning to put my notes and messages into printed form.

Solomon wrote, ". . . of making many books there is no end; and much study is a weariness of the flesh" (Eccl. 12:12). On a sea of books that flood the marketplace, we launch this series of THRU THE BIBLE with the hope that it might draw many to the one Book, *The Bible.*

J. VERNON McGEE

The Book of
ISAIAH

INTRODUCTION

Beginning with Isaiah and continuing through the Old Testament, there is a section of Scripture which is called the prophetic portion of the Bible. That does not mean that prophecy begins with Isaiah, because there are prophecies as far back as the Pentateuch, which was written by Moses. Although the predictive element bulks large in this section, the prophets were more than foretellers. They were men raised up by God in a decadent day when neither priest nor king was a worthy channel through which the expressions of God might flow.

These books of prophecy also contain history, poetry, and law, but their primary message is prophecy. Each writer, from Isaiah to Malachi, is a prophet of God. Today we make an artificial division of the prophets by designating them as the *major prophets* and the *minor prophets*. All of the prophets are in the major league as far as I am concerned—I don't think you can put any of them back in the minors. This artificial division was determined by the length of the book, not by content. Some of the minor prophets are like atom bombs—they may be small, but their content is potent indeed.

These prophets not only spoke of events in the distant future, but they also spoke of local events in the immediate future. They had to speak in this manner in order to qualify for the prophetic office under God according to the Mosaic code. Codes for the priest, the king, and the prophet are given in the Book of Deuteronomy. Note the code for the prophet: "But the prophet, which shall presume to speak a word in my name, which I have not commanded him to speak, or that shall speak in the name of other gods, even that prophet shall die. And if thou say in thine heart, How shall we know the word which the LORD hath not spoken? When a prophet speaketh in the name of the LORD, if the thing follow not, nor come to pass, that is the thing which the LORD hath not spoken, but the prophet hath spoken it presumptuously: thou shalt not be afraid of him" (Deut. 18:20–22). If the local event did not transpire *exactly* as the prophet predicted, he was labeled a false prophet and was so treated. You may be sure that the message of the false prophet is not in the library of inspired Scripture. The prophetic books are filled with events that are local and fulfilled.

If you had lived in Isaiah's day, how would you have known that he was a true prophet? You would have judged him on his local prophecies. He not only spoke of events far in the future, like the first and second comings of Christ, but he also spoke of local things that would happen in the near future. If his local predictions had not come to pass exactly the way they were given, he would have been recognized as a false prophet and stoned.

The prophetic books are filled with local prophecies already fulfilled. All of the prophets gave local prophecies to prove that they were genuine. Remember that a sharp distinction needs to be drawn between fulfilled and unfulfilled prophecy. When any prophecy was first given, it was of course unfulfilled. Since the time the prophecies were given, a great many of them have been fulfilled. One of the greatest evidences that these men were speaking the words of God is that hundreds of their prophecies have been fulfilled—fulfilled literally.

Man cannot guess the future. Even the weatherman has difficulty in prognosticating the weather for twenty-four hours in advance, although he has the advantage of all sorts of scientific and mechanical devices to assist him. The fact of the matter is that no weatherman that you and I listen to so intently would survive as a prophet in Israel!

The law of compound probability forbids man from consistently foretelling the future. Each uncertain element which he adds decreases his chance of accuracy 50 percent. The example of hundreds of prophecies which have had literal fulfillment has a genuine appeal to the honest mind and sincere seeker after the truth. Fulfilled prophecy is one of the infallible proofs of plenary verbal inspiration of Scripture.

Let me illustrate. Suppose I make a prophecy that it is going to rain tomorrow. I would have a fifty-fifty chance of being right. It is either going to rain or it is not going to rain—that is for sure. Now I add another element to my prophecy by predicting that it will begin raining at eleven o'clock in the morning. That reduces my chance of being right another 50 percent, but I still have a 25 percent chance of being correct. But I don't stop there. I not only say that it will start raining at eleven o'clock, but I also say that it will stop raining at three o'clock. I have reduced my chances again and have only a 12½ percent chance of being right. If I keep adding uncertain elements until I have three hundred prophecies, you know they would never be literally fulfilled. No man can guess like that. Only the Holy Spirit of God could give such information. A man would not have a ghost of a chance of being right that many times, and yet God's Word has over three hundred prophecies concerning the first coming of Christ, which have been literally fulfilled.

Why did God give so many prophecies concerning the first coming of Christ to earth? There is a logical and obvious answer. The coming of the Lord Jesus Christ to earth was an important event. God did not want the children of Israel to miss Him. God marked Him out so clearly that Israel had no excuse for not recognizing Him when He was here on this earth.

Let me use a homey illustration. Suppose I am invited to your hometown. You ask me, "When you arrive at the airport, how will I know you?" I would write back and say, "I am arriving at the airport at a certain time on a certain flight. I will be wearing a pair of green-checked trousers and a blue-striped coat. I will have on a big yellow polka dot necktie and a pink shirt with a large purple flower on it. I will be wearing one brown shoe and one black shoe and white socks. On my head you will see a derby hat, and I will be holding a parrot in a cage in one hand, and with the other hand I will be leading a jaguar on a chain." When you arrive at the airport, do you think you would be able to pick me out of the crowd?

When Jesus came to earth more than nineteen hundred years ago, those who had the Old Testament and knew what it said should have been waiting at the inn in Bethlehem or waiting for the news of His birth, because they had all the information they needed. When the wise men appeared, looking for the Lord Jesus, the Israelites at least should have been interested enough to hitch a ride on the back of the camels to take a look themselves. Oh, how tremendously important His coming was, and how clearly God had predicted it!

The prophets were extremely nationalistic. They rebuked sin in high places as well as low places. They warned the nation. They pleaded with a proud people to humble themselves and return to God. Fire and tears were mingled in their message, which was not one of doom and gloom alone, for they saw the Day of the Lord and the glory to follow. All of them looked through the darkness to the dawn of a new day. In the night of sin they saw the light of a coming Savior and Sovereign; they saw the millennial Kingdom coming in all its fullness. Their message must be interpreted before an appreciation of the Kingdom in the New Testament can be attained; the correct perspective of the Kingdom must be gained through the eyes of the Old Testament prophets.

The prophets were not supermen. They were men of passions as we are, but having spoken for God, their message is still the infallible and inspired Word of God. This is substantiated by writers of the New Testament. Peter tells us: "Of which salvation the prophets have inquired and searched diligently, who prophesied of the grace that should come unto you: searching what, or what manner of time the Spirit of Christ which was in them did signify, when it testified beforehand the sufferings of Christ, and the glory that should follow" (1 Pet. 1:10–11).

"Moreover I will endeavour that ye may be able after my decease to have these things always in remembrance. For we have not followed cunningly devised fables, when we made known unto you the power and coming of our Lord Jesus Christ, but were eyewitnesses of his majesty. For he received from God the Father honour and glory, when there came such a voice to him from the excellent glory, This is my beloved Son, in whom I am well pleased. And this voice which came from heaven we heard, when we were with him in the holy mount. We have also a more sure word of prophecy; whereunto ye do well that ye take heed, as unto a light that shineth in a dark place, until the day dawn, and the day star arise in your hearts: knowing this first, that no prophecy of the scripture is of any private interpretation. For the prophecy came not in old time by the will of man: but holy men of God spake as they were moved by the Holy Ghost" (2 Pet. 1:15–21).

It was William Cowper who said, "Sweet is the harp of prophecy; too sweet not to be wronged by a mere mortal touch."

Most of the prophets moved in an orbit of obscurity and anonymity. They did not project their personalities into the prophecy they proclaimed. Jeremiah and Hosea are the exceptions to this, which we will see when we study their books. Isaiah gives us very little history concerning himself. There are a few scant references to his life and ministry. In Isaiah 1:1 he gives the times in which his life was cast: during the reigns of Uzziah, Jotham, Ahaz, and Hezekiah, all kings of Judah. In Isaiah 6 he records his personal call and commission.

The days in which Isaiah prophesied were not the darkest days in Judah internally. Uzziah and Hezekiah were enlightened rulers who sought to serve God, but the days were extremely dark because of the menace of the formidable kingdom of Assyria in the north. The northern kingdom of Israel had already been carried away into captivity.

Isaiah 36—39 records the historical section of the ministry of Isaiah during the crisis when the Assyrian host encompassed Jerusalem. Beyond these few personal sections, Isaiah stands in the shadow as he points to Another who is coming, the One who is the Light of the world.

There are those who believe that Isaiah belonged to the royal family of David. This is supposition and certainly cannot be proven. Likewise it has been stated that he is referred to in Hebrews 11:37 as the one "sawn asunder."

Whether or not this is true, the liberal critic has sawn him asunder as the writer of the book. They have fabricated the ghastly theory that there are several Isaiahs. According to this theory the book was produced by ghostwriters whom they have labeled "Deutero-Isaiah" and "Trito-Isaiah." The book will not yield to being torn apart in this manner, for the New Testament quotes from all sections of the book and gives credit to one Isaiah. The critics have cut up Isaiah like a railroad restaurant pie, but history presents only one Isaiah, not two or three.

A friend of mine, who has made quite a study of the Dead Sea Scrolls, tells me that Isaiah is the scroll the scholars work with the most. There is a great section of Isaiah intact, and only one Isaiah is presented. It is quite interesting that the Lord let a little shepherd boy reach down into a clay pot, in Qumran by the Dead Sea, and pick out a scroll that confounds the critics. The Lord will take care of the critics.

Let me illustrate how ridiculous the double or triple Isaiah hypothesis really is. Suppose a thousand years from today some archaeologists are digging in different parts of the world. One group digs in Kansas, another in Washington, D.C., and another group digs in Europe. They come up with the conclusion that there must have been three Dwight Eisenhowers. There was a General Eisenhower, the military leader of the victorious Allied forces of World War II in the European theater. There was another Eisenhower who was elected president of the United States in 1952 and 1956. There was still another Eisenhower, an invalid and victim of a heart attack and of a serious operation for ileitis. This illustration may seem ridiculous to some people, but that is exactly how I feel when I hear the critics talk about three Isaiahs. Of course there was only one man by the name of Dwight Eisenhower who fulfilled all the requirements without any absurdity. The same is true of Isaiah.

The prophecy of Isaiah is strikingly similar to the organization of the entire Bible. This similarity can be seen in the following comparison:

BIBLE	ISAIAH
66 Books	66 Chapters
39 Books—Old Testament	39 Chapters—Law, Government of God
27 Books—New Testament	27 Chapters—Grace, Salvation of God

There are sixty-six direct quotations from Isaiah in the New Testament. (Some have found eighty-five quotations and allusions to Isaiah in the New Testament.) Twenty of the twenty-seven books of the New

Testament have direct quotations. Isaiah is woven into the New Testament as a brightly colored thread is woven into a beautiful pattern. Isaiah is discernible and conspicuous in the New Testament. Isaiah is chiseled into the rock of the New Testament with the power tool of the Holy Spirit. Isaiah is often used to enforce and enlarge upon the New Testament passages that speak of Christ.

The historic interlude (chs. 36—39) leaves the high plateau of prophecy and drops down to the record of history. Even the form of language is different. It is couched in the form of prose rather than poetry.

The third and last major division (chs. 40—66) returns to the poetic form but is in contrast to the first major section. In the first we had judgment and the righteous government of God; in the last we have the grace of God, the suffering, and the glory to follow. Here all is grace and glory. The opening "Comfort ye" sets the mood and tempo.

It is this section that has caused the liberal critics to postulate the Deutero-Isaiah hypothesis. A change of subject matter does not necessitate a change of authorship. It is interesting that for nineteen hundred years there was not a word about a second Isaiah. John refers to this section as authored by Isaiah (see John 1:23). Our Lord likewise referred to this section as written by Isaiah (see Luke 4:17–21). Philip used a chapter from this section to win an Ethiopian to Christ (see Acts 8). There are numerous other references which confirm the authorship of Isaiah.

Isaiah prophesied many local events. When Jerusalem was surrounded by the Assyrian army, Isaiah made a very daring prophecy: "Therefore thus saith the LORD concerning the king of Assyria, He shall not come into this city, nor shoot an arrow there, nor come before it with shields, nor cast a bank against it" (Isa. 37:33). Also see Isaiah's prophecy concerning the sickness of Hezekiah in Isaiah 38.

There are other prophecies which were not fulfilled in his lifetime, but today they stand fulfilled. See, for instance, his prophecies concerning the city of Babylon: "And Babylon, the glory of kingdoms, the beauty of the Chaldees' excellency, shall be as when God overthrew Sodom and Gomorrah. It shall never be inhabited, neither shall it be dwelt in from generation to generation: neither shall the Arabian pitch tent there; neither shall the shepherds make their fold there. But wild beasts of the desert shall lie there; and their houses shall be full of doleful creatures; and owls shall dwell there, and satyrs shall dance there. And the wild beasts of the islands shall cry in their desolate houses, and dragons in their pleasant palaces: and her time is near to come, and her days shall not be prolonged" (Isa. 13:19–22).

Further fulfillments relative to Babylon are recorded in Isaiah 47. Excavations at Babylon have revealed the accuracy of these prophecies. More than fifty miles of the walls of Babylon have been excavated. The culture of this great civilization is still impressive but lies in dust and debris today according to the written word of Isaiah. This is one of many examples that could be given. Others will come before us in this study as we proceed through the book.

The New Testament presents the Lord Jesus Christ as its theme, and by the same token Isaiah presents the Lord Jesus Christ as his theme. Isaiah has been called the fifth evangelist, and the Book of Isaiah has been called the fifth gospel. Christ's virgin birth, His character, His life, His death, His resurrection, and His second coming are all presented in Isaiah clearly and definitively.

OUTLINE

I. Judgment (Poetry), Chapters 1—35
Revelation of the sovereign on the throne
  A. Solemn Call to the Universe to Come into the Courtroom to Hear God's Charge against the Nation Israel, Chapter 1
  B. Preview of the Future of Judah and Jerusalem, Chapter 2
  C. Present View of Judah and Jerusalem, Chapter 3
  D. Another Preview of the Future, Chapter 4
  E. Parable of the Vineyard and Woes Predicated for Israel, Chapter 5
  F. Isaiah's Personal Call and Commission as Prophet, Chapter 6
  G. Prediction of Local and Far Events, Chapters 7—10
     (Hope of future in coming child)
  H. Millennial Kingdom, Chapters 11—12
  I. Burdens of Surrounding Nations (Largely Fulfilled), Chapters 13—23
     1. Burden of Babylon, Chapters 13—14
     2. Burden of Moab, Chapters 15—16
     3. Burden of Damascus, Chapter 17
     4. Burden of the Land beyond the Rivers of Ethiopia, Chapter 18
     5. Burden of Egypt, Chapters 19—20
     6. Burden of Babylon, Edom, Arabia, Chapter 21
     7. Burden of the Valley of Vision, Chapter 22
     8. Burden of Tyre, Chapter 23
  J. Kingdom, Process, and Program by Which the Throne Is Established on Earth, Chapters 24—34
  K. Kingdom, Mundane Blessings of the Millennium, Chapter 35

II. Historic Interlude (Prose), Chapters 36—39
(This section is probably a prophetic picture of how God will deliver His people in the Great Tribulation, see 2 Kings 18—19; 2 Chron. 29—30.)

HISTORIC INTERLUDE

We have come to the second major division of the Book of Isaiah. This section is unlike that which precedes it and that which follows it. This section leaves the high plateau of prophecy and drops down to the record of history. Even the form of language changes from poetry to prose. The first section dealt with the government of God and the method by which God judges. In the last section we will see the grace of God—salvation instead of judgment. Between these two sections is this historic interlude of four brief chapters. Why are they wedged in between the two major sections of this book? This is a reasonable question which requires investigation and rewards the honest inquirer. There are several significant factors which are worthy of mention.

1. Sacred and secular history are not the same. F. C. Jennings, in his fine work, *Studies in Isaiah*, says, "Divine history is never merely history, never simply a true account of past events." This means that there are great *spiritual* truths couched in sacred history that are seen only by the eye of faith. The Holy Spirit must teach us the divine purpose in recording spiritual history. I want to note several suggested reasons for this:

a. These incidents might seem trite to the average historian who records great world movements, but events that concerned *God's people* were important according to the standards of heaven.

b. These chapters note the transfer of power from Assyria to Babylon. Babylon was the first great world empire and was the real menace to God's people. Babylon was to begin the period designated by our Lord as ". . . the times of the Gentiles . . ." (Luke 21:24).

c. This section is a record of a son of David who was beset by enemies and who went down to the verge of death, but was delivered and continued to reign. In this he foreshadows the great Son of David who was also beset by enemies, was delivered to death, but was raised from the dead, and who is coming again to reign. Hezekiah was only a man who walked in the ways of David, another weak man. Hezekiah lived to play the fool. Our Lord was greater than David, and as the crucified and risen Son of God, He is made unto us ". . . wisdom, and righteousness, and sanctification, and redemption" (1 Cor. 1:30). There are other great spiritual truths which are noted in the chapter outlines.

2. The second significant factor in this historic section is that these particular events are recorded *three* times in Scripture—2 Kings 18—19, 2 Chronicles 29—30, and here in Isaiah. The fact that the Holy Spirit saw fit to record them three times is in itself a matter of great importance. The records are not identical but are similar. Some scholars think that Isaiah is the author of all three, or at least also of the one in the Book of Kings. Surely the Spirit of God has some special truth for us here which should cause us not to hurry over these events as if they were of no great moment.

3. Three significant and stupendous miracles are recorded in this brief section:

a. The death angel slays 185,000 Assyrians (Isa. 37:36–38).

b. The sun retreats ten degrees on the sundial of Ahaz (Isa. 38:7–8).

c. God heals Hezekiah and extends his life fifteen years (Isa. 38:1–5).

4. This section opens with Assyria and closes with Babylon. There are two important letters which Hezekiah received:

a. The first was from Assyria, which Hezekiah took directly to God in prayer. God answered his prayer and delivered His people (Isa. 37:14–20).

b. The second letter was from the king of Babylon, which flattered Hezekiah and which he did not take to the Lord in prayer. As a result, it led to the undoing of Judah (Isa. 39:1–8).

Chapter 36 tells about King Hezekiah and the invasion of Sennacherib, king of Assyria. Chapter 37 tells about King Hezekiah's prayer and the destruction of the Assyrian hosts. Chapter 38 records King Hezekiah's sickness, prayer, and healing. Chapter 39 finds King Hezekiah playing the fool.

CHAPTERS 36 AND 37

THEME: Hezekiah and Assyria

Sennacherib, king of Assyria, had come down like a flood from the north, taking everything in his wake. He had captured every nation and city that stood in his path, or they had capitulated to him. Flushed with victory, he appears with the Assyrian hosts before the walls of Jerusalem. He is surprised and puzzled that Hezekiah would attempt to resist him. He seeks for some explanation, as Hezekiah must have some secret weapon. Rab-shakeh, his representative, ridicules all known possibilities of aid. Arrogantly he demands unconditional surrender. The chapter closes with the terms and threats reported to Hezekiah.

ASSYRIA THREATENS TO INVADE JERUSALEM

Now it came to pass in the fourteenth year of king Hezekiah, that Sennacherib king of Assyria came up against all the defenced cities of Judah, and took them [Isa. 36:1].

You will recall that Isaiah began his prophetic ministry when King Uzziah died, and he continued it through the reigns of Jotham, Ahaz, and now Hezekiah. Hezekiah was one of the five great kings of Judah. During the reigns of these five kings (Asa, Jehoshaphat, Joash, Hezekiah, and Josiah) revival came to the land of Judah. Hezekiah was actually a great king. Second Chronicles 29:1–2 tells us, "Hezekiah began to reign when he was five and twenty years in Jerusalem. And his mother's name was Abijah, the daughter of Zechariah. And he did that which was right in the sight of the LORD, according to all that David his father had done."

Although Hezekiah was a good king, he exhibited weakness when he attempted to stave off the invasion of Jerusalem by bribing Sennacherib (see 2 Kings 18:13–16). He stripped the gold and silver from the temple to meet the exorbitant demands of the king of Assyria. It was to no avail, however, as the army of Assyria was outside the gates of Jerusalem. Payment did not help at all. This policy was not something new then, and it is still with us. Our nation, since World War II, has followed a very weak policy. We have used the almighty dollar to try to buy friends throughout the world, and we don't have many friends today. You cannot get friends by buying them. Our problem is that we haven't learned who our real Friend is. He is the One to whom Hezekiah finally had to turn, the Lord God.

> **And the king of Assyria sent Rab-shakeh from Lachish to Jerusalem unto king Hezekiah with a great army. And he stood by the conduit of the upper pool in the highway of the fuller's field [Isa. 36:2].**

Sennacherib did not condescend to come personally, but instead he sent an army under Rab-shakeh. They are parked now outside the gates of Jerusalem, and General Rab-shakeh is attempting to put fear into the hearts of Hezekiah and the people of Jerusalem so that they will surrender.

Hezekiah sent out a delegation to meet with him.

> **Then came forth unto him Eliakim, Hilkiah's son, which was over the house, and Shebna the scribe, and Joah, Asaph's son, the recorder [Isa. 36:3].**

Hezekiah sent forth this embassage of three to receive the terms offered by Sennacherib.

ASSYRIA DEMANDS SURRENDER OF JERUSALEM

> **And Rab-shakeh said unto them, Say ye now to Hezekiah, Thus saith the great king, the king of Assyria, What confidence is this wherein thou trustest? [Isa. 36:4].**

Rab-shakeh arrogantly expresses surprise that Hezekiah would even dare resist, and he wants to know about the secret weapon in which Hezekiah trusts. He suggests first of all that it might be Egypt.

Lo, thou trustest in the staff of this broken reed, on Egypt; whereon if a man lean, it will go into his hand, and pierce it: so is Pharaoh king of Egypt to all that trust in him [Isa. 36:6].

The Assyrian host was then on the way to Egypt to capture that kingdom and was incensed that Jerusalem blocked the way. The facts were that Hezekiah had hoped for help from Egypt as had Ahaz his father before him. But Hezekiah wouldn't get any help from Egypt—Rab-shakeh was right about that.

Then he suggests another possibility:

But if thou say to me, We trust in the LORD our God: is it not he, whose high places and whose altars Hezekiah hath taken away, and said to Judah and Jerusalem, Ye shall worship before this altar? [Isa. 36:7].

Next Rab-shakeh asks, "Is it true that you are depending upon your God?" Here is where his lack of spiritual discernment gave him a wrong cue. He says, "Don't you know that Hezekiah had all the high places destroyed?" He thought the worship at the heathen altars out yonder on those hilltops was the same as the worship of the living God in Jerusalem. He thought Hezekiah had destroyed the worship of the people so that they had no gods to turn to.

Many people today have no spiritual discernment. Every now and then someone will write to me or say, "All churches are the same. They are all striving to get to the same place." These people are like old Rab-shakeh. They don't seem to know the difference. When they say that it does not make any difference what you believe as long as you are sincere, they contradict the words of our Lord. "Jesus saith unto him, I am the way, the truth, and the life: no man cometh unto the Father, but by me" (John 14:6).

Now the third possibility suggested by Rab-shakeh reveals the haughty attitude of the Assyrian:

> **Now therefore give pledges, I pray thee, to my master the king of Assyria, and I will give thee two thousand horses, if thou be able on thy part to set riders upon them.**
>
> **How then wilt thou turn away the face of one captain of the least of my master's servants, and put thy trust on Egypt for chariots and for horsemen? [Isa. 36:8–9].**

There was the slim possibility that Hezekiah was depending on his own resources and manpower to defend Jerusalem; so Rab-shakeh offers to make things just about equal by giving Hezekiah two thousand horses! He, of course, is ridiculing them.

The fourth possibility suggested by Rab-shakeh is the most subtle of all:

> **And am I now come up without the LORD against this land to destroy it? the LORD said unto me, Go up against this land, and destroy it [Isa. 36:10].**

He suggests that Jehovah of Israel has sent the Assyrian against Jerusalem and that He is therefore on the side of the Assyrian.

It is interesting to note that in World War I the Germans thought God was with them, and we thought God was on our side. I doubt seriously that God was on either side. In this particular case the true God used the Assyrian to destroy His people, but He is not going to let the enemy take Jerusalem.

> **Then said Eliakim and Shebna and Joah unto Rab-shakeh, Speak, I pray thee, unto thy servants in the Syrian language; for we understand it: and speak not to us**

in the Jews' language, in the ears of the people that are
on the wall [Isa. 36:11].

Now Eliakim, Shebna, and Joah ask Rab-shakeh to speak in the Syrian
language. All this time he has been speaking so loudly in the Hebrew
language that the soldiers on the walls of Jerusalem could hear. He
was great at giving out propaganda; enemies always do that. He was
yelling out his ideas at the top of his voice so that the soldiers on the
wall would get the word to the people in Jerusalem; he wanted to get it
past these emissaries. Of course, their protest only caused Rab-
shakeh to talk a little louder.

> Beware lest Hezekiah persuade you, saying, The LORD
> will deliver us. Hath any of the gods of the nations deliv-
> ered his land out of the hand of the king of Assyria?
>
> Where are the gods of Hamath and Arphad? where are
> the gods of Sepharvaim? and have they delivered Sa-
> maria out of my hand?
>
> Who are they among all the gods of these lands, that
> have delivered their land out of my hand, that the
> LORD should deliver Jerusalem out of my hand? [Isa.
> 36:18–20].

Arrogantly Rab-shakeh boasts that none of the gods of other people
have delivered them. Why should the Israelites expect Jehovah to deliver Jerusalem? He placed Jehovah on a par with heathen idols.

REPRESENTATIVES REPORT
ASSYRIA'S BITTER TERMS

Finally the emissaries bring the word to Hezekiah, the king:

> Then came Eliakim, the son of Hilkiah, that was over
> the household, and Shebna the scribe, and Joah, the son

**of Asaph, the recorder, to Hezekiah with their clothes
rent, and told him the words of Rabshakeh [Isa. 36:22].**

The messengers return to report these doleful words to Hezekiah.
    "Clothes" speak of the dignity and glory of man. The saying is that
clothes make the man. Well, "clothes rent" indicates humiliation and
shame. This is a dejected and discouraged delegation that brings to
Hezekiah the message from the king of Assyria.

REACTION OF HEZEKIAH TO THE REPORT

Now notice what Hezekiah does when this report reaches him.

**And it came to pass, when king Hezekiah heard it, that
he rent his clothes, and covered himself with sackcloth,
and went into the house of the LORD [Isa. 37:1].**

His reaction to the report of his messengers reveals a man of faith. In
his extremity he turns to God and goes to the house of the Lord.

**And he sent Eliakim, who was over the household, and
Shebna the scribe, and the elders of the priests covered
with sackcloth, unto Isaiah the prophet the son of Amoz
[Isa. 37:2].**

Hezekiah now sends his messengers to Isaiah the prophet. This is another act of faith. He wants a word from God.

**And they said unto him, Thus saith Hezekiah, This day
is a day of trouble, and of rebuke, and of blasphemy: for
the children are come to the birth, and there is not
strength to bring forth [Isa. 37:3].**

The message to Isaiah is ominous, black, and pessimistic. It is a day of
trouble, rebuke, and blasphemy.

> It may be the LORD thy God will hear the words of Rab-
> shakeh, whom the king of Assyria his master hath sent
> to reproach the living God, and will reprove the words
> which the LORD thy God hath heard: wherefore lift up
> thy prayer for the remnant that is left [Isa. 37:4].

He speaks of the Lord as "thy God," not as "our God." Why didn't he say "our God" to begin with? However, he will correct this in his prayer in verse 20.

ENCOURAGEMENT FROM THE LORD
THROUGH ISAIAH

> So the servants of king Hezekiah came to Isaiah.

> And Isaiah said unto them, Thus shall ye say unto your
> master, Thus saith the LORD, Be not afraid of the words
> that thou hast heard, wherewith the servants of the king
> of Assyria have blasphemed me [Isa. 37:5-6].

God gives assurance to Hezekiah that the blasphemy of the Assyrian has not escaped His attention. Likewise, God cannot, nor will not, ignore it.

> Behold, I will send a blast upon him, and he shall hear
> a rumour, and return to his own land; and I will cause
> him to fall by the sword in his own land [Isa. 37:7].

He would not be killed near Jerusalem but in his own land. This had literal fulfillment, as we shall see. God declares the destruction of Assyria.

THREATENING LETTER TO HEZEKIAH

When Rab-shakeh got back to his army, he learned that the king of Assyria had left Lachish and was going to war against Libnah. A rumor came that the main force of the Assyrian army was being attacked by the Egyptian army. Rab-shakeh withdrew from Jerusalem temporarily to assist the main force of the Assyrian army, but to "save face" he dispatched a letter from Sennacherib to Hezekiah saying, "I'll be back!"

The message of the letter was another attempt to shake Hezekiah's faith in God's deliverance.

> **Thus shall ye speak to Hezekiah king of Judah, saying, Let not thy God, in whom thou trustest, deceive thee, saying, Jerusalem shall not be given into the hand of the king of Assyria [Isa. 37:10].**

He repeats the same words of Rab-shakeh.

> **Behold, thou hast heard what the kings of Assyria have done to all lands by destroying them utterly; and shalt thou be delivered?**

> **Have the gods of the nations delivered them which my fathers have destroyed, as Gozan, and Haran, and Rezeph, and the children of Eden which were in Telassar? [Isa. 37:11–12].**

Here he goes beyond the former word and boasts that no gods of any nation had delivered their people out of the hand of the Assyrian.

> **Where is the king of Hamath, and the king of Arphad, and the king of the city of Sepharvaim, Hena, and Ivah? [Isa. 37:13].**

He quotes historical facts that were difficult to answer.

HEZEKIAH'S PRAYER

Now notice the action of Hezekiah—I love this!

> And Hezekiah received the letter from the hand of the
> messengers, and read it: and Hezekiah went up unto the
> house of the LORD, and spread it before the LORD [Isa.
> 37:14].

When Hezekiah received the letter, he went to God directly and spread
the letter before Him. Then follows one of the truly great prayers of
Scripture.

> And Hezekiah prayed unto the LORD, saying,

> O LORD of hosts, God of Israel, that dwellest between the
> cherubims, thou art the God, even thou alone, of all the
> kingdoms of the earth: thou hast made heaven and earth
> [Isa. 37:15–16].

No instructed Israelites believed that God was a *local* deity who dwelt
in the temple—just a little box in Jerusalem! King Solomon had
prayed: "But will God indeed dwell on the earth? behold, the heaven
and heaven of heavens cannot contain thee; how much less this house
that I have builded" (1 Kings 8:27). Every Israelite recognized that He
was the God of heaven, the Creator of heaven and earth.

Hezekiah pleads with Him to hear and deliver His people from the
threatening Assyrian:

> Incline thine ear, O LORD, and hear; open thine eyes, O
> LORD, and see: and hear all the words of Sennacherib,
> which hath sent to reproach the living God [Isa. 37:17].

Hezekiah shows God the letter and calls attention to the fact that it is
directly against God.

> Of a truth, LORD, the kings of Assyria have laid waste all
> the nations, and their countries,

> And have cast their gods into the fire: for they were no
> gods, but the work of men's hands, wood and stone:
> therefore they have destroyed them [Isa. 37:18–19].

Hezekiah acknowledges the truth of the letter. There was no need to deny or ignore it. When we deal with God, it is wise to tell Him the truth, especially about ourselves, and not try to conceal anything.

> **Now therefore, O Lord our God, save us from his hand, that all the kingdoms of the earth may know that thou art the Lord, even thou only [Isa. 37:20].**

GOD'S ANSWER THROUGH ISAIAH

God says that He has heard the blasphemy of the Assyrian. Notice how He will deal with him:

> **Because thy rage against me, and thy tumult, is come up into mine ears, therefore will I put my hook in thy nose, and my bridle in thy lips, and I will turn thee back by the way by which thou camest [Isa. 37:29].**

Now God gives this word of comfort and assurance to His people.

> **And this shall be a sign unto thee, Ye shall eat this year such as groweth of itself; and the second year that which springeth of the same: and in the third year sow ye, and reap, and plant vineyards, and eat the fruit thereof [Isa. 37:30].**

The primary thought is that the children of Judah would continue on in the land a little longer.

Note the boldness of this prophecy:

> **Therefore thus saith the Lord concerning the king of Assyria, He shall not come into this city, nor shoot an arrow there, nor come before it with shields, nor cast a bank against it [Isa. 37:33].**

If one of the 185,000 Assyrians had accidentally shot an arrow over the walls of Jerusalem, God's Word would have been inaccurate! How wonderful are the promises of God!

By the way that he came, by the same shall he return, and shall not come into this city, saith the LORD [Isa. 37:34].

This is specific and was also literally fulfilled.

GOD DESTROYS THE ASSYRIAN ARMY

Then the angel of the LORD went forth, and smote in the camp of the Assyrians a hundred and fourscore and five thousand: and when they arose early in the morning, behold, they were all dead corpses [Isa. 37:36].

In the morning the men who were stationed on the walls of Jerusalem saw an amazing sight! The enemies they so feared were now lifeless corpses.

So Sennacherib king of Assyria departed, and went and returned, and dwelt at Nineveh [Isa. 37:37].

Now let's see what happened to the king of Assyria.

And it came to pass, as he was worshipping in the house of Nisroch his god, that Adrammelech and Sharezer his sons smote him with the sword; and they escaped into the land of Armenia: and Esarhaddon his son reigned in his stead [Isa. 37:38].

Secular history confirms the fact that Sennacherib was murdered by his sons. It was about this time that the great kingdom of Assyria began to disintegrate and eventually was taken over by Babylon. God had already let Isaiah know that He was preparing a kingdom down on the banks of the Euphrates River, which would be the one to take the southern kingdom into captivity. God knew that though He delivered His people by this tremendous miracle in the days of Hezekiah, soon the day would return when He again would say, "Ah sinful nation, a people laden with iniquity, a seed of evildoers, children that are corrupters: they have forsaken the Lord, they have provoked the Holy One of Israel unto anger, they are gone away backward" [Isa. 1:4].

CHAPTER 38

THEME: Prayer of Hezekiah when told he is to die; promise of healing—miracle of the sundial; Hezekiah's poem of praise

This chapter deals with King Hezekiah's illness, prayer, and healing. It is well to keep in mind that while Hezekiah was beset by the danger of the Assyrian host, he was plagued by a "boil." His deliverance from death must have been prior to the destruction of the Assyrian host. It was while the siege was going on, and the answer to prayer must have encouraged his heart relative to Isaiah's prediction of the coming deliverance of Jerusalem. Hezekiah reigned twenty-nine years. He reigned fifteen years after this event, so his sickness was in the fourteenth year of his reign, and we are told that Sennacherib came up against Jerusalem in the fourteenth year of Hezekiah's reign (see Isa. 36:1). All of this happened in the same year—the sickness of Hezekiah and the siege of Jerusalem by the Assyrians.

PRAYER OF HEZEKIAH WHEN TOLD HE IS TO DIE

In those days was Hezekiah sick unto death. And Isaiah the prophet the son of Amoz came unto him, and said unto him, Thus saith the LORD, Set thine house in order: for thou shalt die, and not live [Isa. 38:1].

It is interesting the way this chapter opens. We have seen that "in that day" is a technical expression that speaks of the Tribulation and millennial days. This verse does not open by saying, "In that day," but by saying, "In those days." What "days" is Isaiah talking about? He is talking about those days in which he and Hezekiah lived. Hezekiah was sick unto death. He was having trouble with a "boil" that was just about to kill him. On top of that he was having trouble with the Assyrians. There are those who believe that Hezekiah's "boil" was either cancer or leprosy, or something similar. Whatever it was, it was a terminal disease, and his time to die had come.

The sentence of death was delivered to Hezekiah by Isaiah. It is true that this sentence of death rests upon each one of us, although we do not know the day nor the hour. But we do know this: ". . . it is appointed unto men once to die, but after this the judgment" (Heb. 9:27). This is a divine date. If each one of us knew the exact time, our life-style would change.

Some years ago I received a letter from a fine young minister who had been told by his doctor that he had cancer and that his days were limited. He sent out a letter to some of his friends, and I was privileged to be included in that list. Here is a brief quotation from his letter so that you might know the thinking of a man under the shadow of death: "One thing I have discovered in the last few days. When a Christian is suddenly confronted with a sentence of death, he surely begins to give a proper evaluation of material things. My fishing gear and books and orchard are not nearly so valuable as they were a week ago." I conducted this young preacher's funeral. And many years later I had the experience of having cancer myself. My doctor told me he thought I had only about three months to live. I can bear witness to the accuracy of the young preacher's statement. It was amazing how certain things suddenly became very unimportant. One of those things was my home. I thought I would not be living in it but a few more weeks, and it certainly became unimportant to me; but where I was going became very important. Well, God had other plans for me, for which I am indeed grateful. I thank and praise Him for each new day He gives to me.

When Hezekiah was confronted with death, what did he do?

Then Hezekiah turned his face toward the wall, and prayed unto the LORD [Isa. 38:2].

We have seen Hezekiah in prayer before when he spread Sennacherib's letter before the Lord.

And said, Remember now, O Lord, I beseech thee, how I have walked before thee in truth and with a perfect heart, and have done that which is good in thy sight. And Hezekiah wept sore [Isa. 38:3].

This is a time when a man can weep. I wept when I was told I was going to die. I am sure the young preacher wept when he heard the news from his doctor. You are bound to weep at a time like that. But Hezekiah also prayed on the basis of his life. This man had a good reputation before God, and under the Mosaic Law this was the accurate thing to do. Second Kings 18:5 says concerning Hezekiah: "He trusted in the Lord God of Israel; so that after him was none like him among all the kings of Judah, nor any that were before him." Hezekiah was an outstanding man. He was not boasting when he made that claim.

PROMISE OF HEALING—MIRACLE
OF THE SUNDIAL

Then came the word of the Lord to Isaiah, saying,

Go, and say to Hezekiah, Thus saith the Lord, the God of David thy father, I have heard thy prayer, I have seen thy tears: behold, I will add unto thy days fifteen years [Isa. 38:4–5].

God did hear and answer his prayer and extended his life by fifteen years. He did it, not for Hezekiah's sake, but for David's sake.

That is not the basis upon which our prayers are heard today. Our prayers are heard for the sake of David's greater Son, the Lord Jesus Christ. In John 16:23–24 the Lord says, "And in that day ye shall ask me nothing. Verily, verily, I say unto you, Whatsoever ye shall ask the Father in my name, he will give it you. Hitherto have ye asked nothing in my name: ask, and ye shall receive, that your joy may be full" (italics mine). You and I can go to our Heavenly Father with our requests in the name of Christ. To pray in the *name* of Christ means that you are in Christ, and you are praying for His will to be done. It means that it is to please Him. Sometimes He will heal and sometimes He won't. He is the One to decide.

> **And I will deliver thee and this city out of the hand of the king of Assyria: and I will defend this city [Isa. 38:6].**

God ties in His deliverance of Jerusalem from the Assyrian with the deliverance of Hezekiah from death. God's answer to one request will encourage the believer's heart that He will answer the other requests. To be honest with you, I have been greatly strengthened in my own faith since God heard and answered the prayers of a host of radio listeners concerning my health.

> **And this shall be a sign unto thee from the LORD, that the LORD will do this thing that he hath spoken;**
>
> **Behold, I will bring again the shadow of the degrees, which is gone down in the sun dial of Ahaz, ten degrees backward. So the sun returned ten degrees, by which degrees it was gone down [Isa. 38:7–8].**

God gave him a sign, which was an assurance that He would answer his prayer.

F. C. Jennings (*Studies in Isaiah*, p. 438) translates the verse like this: "Behold, I will cause the shadow of the steps to return, which is gone down on the steps of Ahaz with the sun, backward ten steps. And the sun returned ten steps by the steps which it had gone down." You see, the translation of "degrees" can also be "steps." Dr. Jennings comments: "We can now transport ourselves in spirit to Hezekiah's palace, and into his chamber. There lies the king, still prone on his couch, but with his face no longer turned to the wall, but joy and hope brightening his eye as he looks out of the window to the gardens, in the midst of which, and in full view, stands an obelisk, or column, with a series of steps leading up to it, and at least ten of these are lying in the column's shadow; for the sun has gone so far down as to throw the shadow over that number of steps. But look again, the once darkened steps are now in clearest sunlight—'tis the sign for which the king had asked!"

HEZEKIAH'S POEM OF PRAISE

The writing of Hezekiah king of Judah, when he had been sick, and was recovered of his sickness [Isa. 38:9].

The verses following are a fine thesis on death by one who was very near to it. Many believe that Hezekiah composed Psalm 116 at this time.

Now the question arises: Was Hezekiah right in asking God to extend his life?

The LORD was ready to save me: therefore we will sing my songs to the stringed instruments all the days of our life in the house of the LORD [Isa. 38:20].

At this time there was a great welling up of praise in the heart of Hezekiah. His song of praise to God was evidently set to music and sung.

However, after this experience Hezekiah became rather proud and arrogant. In the Book of Chronicles, which is God's viewpoint of history, we are told: "But Hezekiah rendered not again according to the benefit done unto him; for his heart was lifted up: therefore there was wrath upon him, and upon Judah and Jerusalem" (2 Chron. 32:25). Here is evidence to the fact that maybe he should not have asked for an extension of life because it led to pride in his life—he was raised up!

When I became ill, I remembered the story of Hezekiah. I went to the Lord and said, "If you will let me live, I will promise to do your will, and I will continue to get out your Word." That is the reason I have overextended myself in conferences and meetings. I didn't want to let the Lord down. But He has made it pretty clear to me that I should not kill myself by overdoing, since He has extended my life. Now I am trying to be reasonable in what I do.

After experiencing a miracle like Hezekiah did, there is a danger of withdrawing from the Lord. You would think that it would draw one closer to Him, but instead there is a grave danger of getting away from Him.

Was he right in asking God to extend his life? Should he not have died when the time came? There is another consideration which leads me to believe that he should have died when he was so ill. Manasseh, his son, was twelve years old when he began to reign, which means that he was born after Hezekiah's sickness. Manasseh was the worst king who reigned in either kingdom. I consider Manasseh worse than Ahab and Jezebel put together. I think that it was during his reign that the Shekinah glory departed. If it didn't depart during his reign, I can't think of any reason it would depart afterward. Manasseh was very much like Antichrist, the Man of Sin who is yet to come.

In the next chapter we will see that Hezekiah played the fool after his experience in healing.

Now *how* did God perform the healing of Hezekiah? Did he have Isaiah pray over him? Or did Isaiah lay his hand on him so hard that he fell backward? No. Notice what Isaiah did—

For Isaiah had said, Let them take a lump of figs, and lay it for a plaster upon the boil, and he shall recover [Isa. 38:21].

In other words, he did the two things that James recommends: "Is any sick among you? let him call for the elders of the church; and let them pray over him, anointing him with oil in the name of the Lord" (James 5:14). This anointing is not religious nor ceremonial. The oil is for healing; it is medicinal. And the elders are to pray for the one who is sick. What God said through Isaiah and through James is the same. When you get sick, pray and call for the doctor. God expects us to be sensible.

CHAPTER 39

THEME: Hezekiah and Babylon

The transfer of the enemy of Judah from Assyria to Babylon is one of the outstanding features of this section. At this time Babylon was a struggling city on the banks of the Euphrates, unable to overcome Assyria. However, Babylon was to become the great head of gold in the times of the Gentiles, and that makes this chapter significant.

This chapter reveals the great blunder of Hezekiah's life and also his human frailty and weakness. It is after the hour of great spiritual triumph that our worst defeats come.

HEZEKIAH RECEIVES THE BABYLONIAN EMBASSAGE

At that time Merodach-baladan, the son of Baladan, king of Babylon, sent letters and a present to Hezekiah: for he had heard that he had been sick, and was recovered [Isa. 39:1].

Merodach-baladan is a meaningless king to us, but his name is full of meaning. F. C. Jennings calls our attention to the fact that *Merodach* means "a rebel" and *baladan* means "not the Lord." Behind this king, of course, is Nimrod, the founder of Babylon, and Satan, who is the archrebel against God and is the "god of this world."

These ambassadors brought a letter which flattered Hezekiah. They said, "The king of Babylon has been concerned about you. He heard that you were sick and have recovered; so he sends a gift to rejoice with you."

And Hezekiah was glad of them, and shewed them the house of his precious things, the silver, and the gold, and the spices, and the precious ointment, and all the

**house of his armour, and all that was found in his trea-
sures: there was nothing in his house, nor in all his do-
minion, that Hezekiah shewed them not [Isa. 39:2].**

At this time Hezekiah had not lost very many of the riches that David
and Solomon had gathered. He made the mistake of showing his silver
and gold, for he was immensely wealthy. We are told in 2 Chronicles
32:27–28, "And Hezekiah had exceeding much riches and honour:
and he made himself treasuries for silver, and for gold, and for precious stones, and for spices, and for shields, and for all manner of
pleasant jewels; storehouses also for the increase of corn, and wine,
and oil; and stalls for all manner of beasts, and cotes for flocks."

It is interesting how Hezekiah received the embassage from Babylon. They gave him a gift and a get-well card from the king. Instead
of taking the letter and opening it before the Lord like he did the letter
from the Assyrians, he just put it aside. They had flattered him, and so
he gave the visitors the VIP treatment. He took them on a tour of the
grounds of Jerusalem. Solomon had cornered the world's gold market,
and he had also cornered the market on quite a few other things. All of
it was stored away in Jerusalem. Hezekiah foolishly showed this great
wealth to his visitors, who went back to their king and told him that
when he was strong enough, they knew where he could get all of the
gold, silver, and jewels that he would need to carry on warfare.

Hezekiah made a big mistake, and Isaiah heard about what he had
done.

**Then came Isaiah the prophet unto king Hezekiah, and
said unto him, What said these men? and from whence
came they unto thee? And Hezekiah said, They are come
from a far country unto me, even from Babylon [Isa.
39:3].**

Hezekiah thought it was wonderful, but Isaiah recognized the danger.

**Then said he, What have they seen in thine house? And
Hezekiah answered, All that is in mine house have they**

seen: there is nothing among my treasures that I have not shewed them [Isa. 39:4].

It was a very foolish thing that Hezekiah had done.

Then said Isaiah to Hezekiah, Hear the word of the LORD of hosts:

Behold, the days come, that all that is in thine house, and that which thy fathers have laid up in store until this day, shall be carried to Babylon: nothing shall be left, saith the LORD.

And of thy sons that shall issue from thee, which thou shalt beget, shall they take away; and they shall be eunuchs in the palace of the king of Babylon [Isa. 39:5–7].

Hezekiah played the fool. He should never have shown his treasures to strangers. Isaiah's prophecy was literally fulfilled (see 2 Kings 24—25; Dan. 1).

Then said Hezekiah to Isaiah, Good is the word of the LORD which thou hast spoken. He said moreover, For there shall be peace and truth in my days [Isa. 39:8].

Hezekiah's reply to Isaiah is very strange. He said in effect, "I am glad this prophecy won't take place in my day." He was grateful that these things would not come to pass in his days, but what about his children and grandchildren and great-grandchildren? It did take place in their day.

Hezekiah's life was extended for fifteen years. Was it good? It was not good. He lived to play the fool. Three terrible things took place during those years.

This chapter concludes the historic section.

CHAPTER 40

THEME: Comfort, a message from God; creation, a revelation of God; consideration, a call from God

Chapter 40 brings us to the final major division of the Book of Isaiah. There is a sharp contrast between the first and last sections of this book. The first section was a revelation of the *Sovereign* upon the throne, while this final section is a revelation of the *Savior* in the place of suffering. In chapter 6 we saw the *crown*; in chapter 53 we shall see the *cross*. The theme in the first section was the *government* of God; in this section it is the *grace* of God.

The opening words, "Comfort ye," set the mood and tempo for this final section. The message from God is comfort rather than the judgment which we saw in the first section.

The change of subject matter has led the liberal critic to postulate the Deutero-Isaiah hypothesis. Because the subjects are entirely different, they suppose that they were written by different writers—two Isaiahs. Well, a change of message certainly does not necessitate a change of authorship. The message has changed but not the messenger. Many authors write on subjects that are entirely different. For example, I have a booklet on Psalm 2, which is God's judgment, and one on Psalm 22, which is God's salvation—two entirely different subjects, but written by the same individual.

In this section of Isaiah the thunder and lightning of Sinai are subdued, smothered by the wonderful message of grace which comes from God.

COMFORT, A MESSAGE FROM GOD

Comfort ye, comfort ye my people, saith your God [Isa. 40:1].

All of the "woes" and the "burdens" of the first section have been lifted because there is now a burden-bearer, One who later on will fulfill everything that Isaiah said about Him. He will be the One to give the invitation, "Come unto me, all ye that labour and are heavy laden, and I will give you rest" (Matt. 11:28). The Lord Jesus Christ lifts burdens.

"C᾿mfort ye, comfort ye" is a sign of yearning from the pulsating heart of God. Our God is the God of "all comfort." That is the way Paul speaks of Him in 2 Corinthians 1:3–4: "Blessed be God, even the Father of our Lord Jesus Christ, the Father of mercies, and the God of all comfort; Who comforteth us in all our tribulation, that we may be able to comfort them which are in any trouble, by the comfort wherewith we ourselves are comforted of God." The Holy Spirit is called "the Comforter." The Lord Jesus said, "And I will pray the Father, and he shall give you another Comforter, that he may abide with you for ever" (John 14:16). He is today *our* Comforter.

Speak ye comfortably to Jerusalem, and cry unto her, that her warfare is accomplished, that her iniquity is pardoned: for she hath received of the LORD's hand double for all her sins [Isa. 40:2].

It has been suggested that when there was an indebtedness or mortgage on a house in Israel, the fact was written on a paper, a legal document, and put on the doorpost so that all their neighbors and friends would know that they had a mortgage on their place. Another copy was kept by the one who held the mortgage. When the debt was paid, the second copy, the carbon copy, was nailed over the other doorpost so that all might see that the debt was paid. This is the meaning of "she hath received of the LORD's hand double for all her sins." The sins of Jerusalem were paid for by the One who suffered outside her gates. This is the difference between the dealings of God with His people in the Old Testament and with us in our day. It actually separates Christianity from all pagan religions and from the Mosaic Law. The difference is all wrapped up in that little word *propitiation*. In the heathen religions the people bring an offering to their gods to appease them, and that is what *propitiation* means. Many people think that that is what it means in the Bible, that they have to "do" something—

because God is angry—to win Him over. The people in heathen religions are always doing that because their gods are always angry and difficult to get along with. Their feelings are easily hurt, and they are not very friendly. The fact is that sin, man's sin, has alienated him from God, but it is *God* who did something. And today God is propitious. You don't have to do anything to win Him over. *Propitiation* is toward God, and *reconciliation* is toward us. God has done everything that needs to be done. Today *we* are asked to be reconciled to God, not to do something to win Him over. God is already won over; that is what Jesus Christ did for us on the cross. We need only accept what Christ has done. This is the word of comfort for a lost world today.

> **The voice of him that crieth in the wilderness, Prepare
> ye the way of the Lord, make straight in the desert a
> highway for our God [Isa. 40:3].**

All four writers of the Gospel records—Matthew, Mark, Luke, and John—quote this verse as applying to John the Baptist. Since it appears four times in the New Testament, I'm not going to argue about it. I say that it refers to John the Baptist.

> **Every valley shall be exalted, and every mountain and
> hill shall be made low: and the crooked shall be made
> straight, and the rough places plain:**
>
> **And the glory of the Lord shall be revealed, and all flesh
> shall see it together: for the mouth of the Lord hath spoken it.**
>
> **The voice said, Cry. And he said, What shall I cry? All
> flesh is grass, and all the goodliness thereof is as the
> flower of the field [Isa. 40:4–6].**

Luke quotes this as applying to John the Baptist.

> **The grass withereth, the flower fadeth: because the
> spirit of the Lord bloweth upon it: surely the people is
> grass.**

The grass withereth, the flower fadeth: but the word of our God shall stand for ever [Isa. 40:7–8].

Man is compared to the grass of the field. The question is, How can there be comfort in being reminded that we are like grass? Hence in California grass is beautiful after the spring rain; but not many weeks later, after the sun has beat upon it for awhile, it begins to wither and die. Man is just like that.

You say, "Well there is no comfort in that!" Yes, there is. Man is faint, frail, and feeble, but the Word of God is strong, sure, and secure. God's Word is our hiding place, a foundation upon which we can rest; it is our sword and buckler, high tower, protection, security, and salvation. In 1 Peter 1:23–25 we read, "Being born again, not of corruptible seed, but of incorruptible, by the word of God, which liveth and abideth for ever. For all flesh is as grass, and all the glory of man as the flower of grass. The grass withereth, and the flower thereof falleth away: but the word of the LORD endureth for ever. And this is the word which by the gospel is preached unto you." It is only the gospel that gives eternal life to man who naturally is just a transitory creature on this earth.

Now note the wonderful message—

O Zion, that bringest good tidings, get thee up into the high mountain; O Jerusalem, that bringest good tidings, lift up thy voice with strength; lift it up, be not afraid; say unto the cities of Judah, Behold your God! [Isa. 40:9].

"Good tidings" is the gospel, and the "good tidings" of John the Baptist was "Behold your God!" Until you have seen Jesus Christ as God manifest in the flesh, you haven't really seen Him. You must come to Him as He is—not just as a Man, but as God, Immanuel, God with us. If He is just a human, He cannot be my Savior; but He is *Immanuel*, and He is my Savior. How wonderful this is!

> Behold the Lord GOD will come with strong hand, and
> his arm shall rule for him: behold, his reward is with
> him, and his work before him [Isa. 40:10].

Now Isaiah, as he generally does, draws together the first and second comings of Christ. This verse looks forward to His second coming. Actually, the gospel includes both the first and second comings of Christ. We are apt to get sidetracked and put all the emphasis on Jesus' first coming or on His second coming. Well, let's put our emphasis on both comings, which is the totality of the gospel.

> He shall feed his flock like a shepherd: he shall gather
> the lambs with his arm, and carry them in his bosom,
> and shall gently lead those that are with young [Isa.
> 40:11].

The Lord Jesus took the title of Shepherd when He came the first time. "I am the good shepherd: the good shepherd giveth his life for the sheep" (John 10:11). He also said, ". . . I lay down my life for the sheep" (John 10:15).

CREATION, A REVELATION OF GOD

The next verse introduces the section that speaks of the greatness of God as Creator.

> Who hath measured the waters in the hollow of his
> hand, and meted out heaven with the span, and compre-
> hended the dust of the earth in a measure, and weighed
> the mountains in scales, and the hills in a balance? [Isa.
> 40:12].

Who has done that? To begin with, when you get out into space, you don't weigh anything; so who is doing the weighing today, and where is it going to be weighed? This verse makes me feel like singing "How Great Thou Art"!

> **Who hath directed the spirit of the LORD, or being his counsellor hath taught him?**
>
> **With whom took he counsel, and who instructed him, and taught him in the path of judgment, and taught him knowledge, and shewed to him the way of understanding? [Isa. 40:13–14].**

God knows no equal nor is there anyone to whom He can go for advice. Someone has asked the rather facetious question, "What is it that you have seen that God has never seen?" The answer is very simple. God has never seen His equal. I see mine every day.

> **To whom then will ye liken God? or what likeness will ye compare unto him? [Isa. 40:18].**

You and I know very little. All we know is what He has revealed in the Word of God, and I don't think He has told us everything. To begin with, we can't even comprehend what He *has* told us.

Isaiah is contrasting God to idols. "To whom then will ye liken God? or what likeness will ye compare unto him?" Look around you at the pictures of Him. Personally, I don't care for any pictures of Jesus because they are *not* pictures of Jesus. I don't become very popular when I say this. Stores that sell such pictures and people who are rather sentimental think I am terrible. But, my friend, we don't need pictures of Him. I agree with the old Scottish philosopher who said years ago, "Men never thought of painting a picture of Jesus until they had lost His presence in their hearts."

Now here is the first rather ironical attack that Isaiah will make against idolatry—

> **The workman melteth a graven image, and the goldsmith spreadeth it over with gold, and casteth silver chains [Isa. 40:19].**

The rich make a very ornate idol. They have a rich god.

> He that is so impoverished that he hath no oblation
> chooseth a tree that will not rot; he seeketh unto him a
> cunning workman to prepare a graven image, that shall
> not be moved [Isa. 40:20].

The poor can have only a crude idol; he whittles out a god from a
piece of wood. How preposterous idolatry is!

> Have ye not known? have ye not heard? hath it not been
> told you from the beginning? have ye not understood
> from the foundations of the earth? [Isa. 40:21].

It is utterly ridiculous to compare God to some dumb idol.

> It is he that sitteth upon the circle of the earth, and the
> inhabitants thereof are as grasshoppers; that stretcheth
> out the heavens as a curtain, and spreadeth them out as
> a tent to dwell in [Isa. 40:22].

The Old Testament does not teach that the earth is flat; but scientists
in the days of Columbus taught this theory. Those so-called scientists
did not pay attention to the Word of God in that day, and they missed
something. And I think scientists are missing something today. It is
clearly stated in this verse that the earth is a sphere, a circle posi-
tioned in an even greater universe, and that God's throne is far beyond
the penetration of the most powerful telescopes as they search out the
limitless vault of space.

CONSIDERATION, A CALL FROM GOD

In the light of all of this, God calls us to consider.

> Why sayest thou, O Jacob, and speakest, O Israel, My
> way is hid from the LORD, and my judgment is passed
> over from my God? [Isa. 40:27].

God *knows* about the difficulties and problems of His people. If you belong to Him, He is able to quiet the storms of life, but sometimes there are lessons for His own to learn in the storm. When you find yourself in the midst of a storm, instead of sitting and weeping and criticizing God, why don't you look around and find out what lesson He wants you to learn? God will not let you go through trials unless He has something for you to learn.

The lesson may be this:

> **Hast thou not known? hast thou not heard, that the everlasting God, the LORD, the Creator of the ends of the earth, fainteth not, neither is weary? there is no searching of his understanding [Isa. 40:28].**

We have a great God. He never gets tired. He is not like man.

> **Even the youths shall faint and be weary, and the young men shall utterly fall:**

> **But they that wait upon the LORD shall renew their strength; they shall mount up with wings as eagles; they shall run, and not be weary; and they shall walk, and not faint [Isa. 40:30–31].**

There are three degrees of power here, and several expositors have likened them to the three stages of Christian growth that you have in 1 John 2:12–14. These three stages of growth are: (1) the young Christian shall mount up as an eagle; (2) the adult Christian shall run; and (3) the mature Christian shall walk.

This reminds me of the black preacher down in my southland who preached a very wonderful sermon, in which he said, "Brethren, this church, it needs to walk." And one of the deacons said, "Amen." He continued, "Brethren, this church needs to run." And the deacon said, "Hallelujah." Then he said, "Brethren, this church needs to fly." And this deacon said, "Amen and hallelujah." Then the minister said,

"Well, it's going to cost money to make this church fly." To this the deacon replied, "Let her walk, brother, let her walk."

My friend, regardless of who you are, if you are going to move with God through this earth, it will cost you something. But God will furnish you strength whatever your condition. If you need strength to walk, He will give it to you. If you need strength to fly, He has that for you also. This is a wonderful chapter revealing the comfort of God as our Creator, as our Savior, and as our Sustainer.

CHAPTER 41

THEME: God overrules individuals; God invites Israel
to trust Him; God overturns idols

This chapter continues the thought of chapter 40 in setting forth the greatness of God. The emphasis here is not upon God as Creator so much as upon His *dealings* with man. The greatness of God is revealed in both creation and human history.

There are also some things in this chapter that are rather enigmatic. It seems that there is a bare profile of prophecy in the background, but the theme is that God will protect and lead His children through the world which is fraught with pitfalls and dangers. Therefore, comfort is here for the child of God.

GOD OVERRULES INDIVIDUALS

Keep silence before me, O islands; and let the people renew their strength: let them come near; then let them speak: let us come near together to judgment [Isa. 41:1].

The whole world of individuals is moving toward judgment.

The showdown is coming between light and darkness, between God and mammon, between faith and unbelief. God is now calling upon individuals to turn to Him and accept the salvation He has to offer. God is propitious. He is not demanding anything of you. He is simply asking you to accept the grace and salvation that He has to offer.

Who raised up the righteous man from the east, called him to his foot, gave the nations before him, and made him rule over kings? he gave them as the dust to his sword, and as driven stubble to his bow [Isa. 41:2].

"Righteous man from the east" is a strong expression. There are those who feel that this is a veiled suggestion of Cyrus. Cyrus will be mentioned by name shortly, but this is not the place. I believe that the word actually refers to a quality—*righteousness*—rather than to a person. It could be a reference to the rule of righteousness which Christ will establish at His return to earth. We find this thought developed in this section.

> **They helped every one his neighbour; and every one said to his brother, Be of good courage [Isa. 41:6].**

Since God is coming to right the wrongs and relieve injustices, individuals who are right with God can be of good courage. There is hope for the little man who trusts God. He doesn't have to worry about the future.

GOD INVITES ISRAEL TO TRUST HIM

Here again we have a reference to idolatry.

> **So the carpenter encouraged the goldsmith, and he that smootheth with the hammer him that smote the anvil, saying, It is ready for the soldering: and he fastened it with nails, that it should not be moved [Isa. 41:7].**

In an emergency some folk hammered themselves out a god, that is, a temporary idol. But now God says:

> **But thou, Israel, art my servant, Jacob whom I have chosen, the seed of Abraham my friend [Isa. 41:8].**

God now turns to Israel to comfort them in their distress. God says, "Instead of hammering out an idol, why not turn to Me?" After all, He knows they are sinners. He still calls them Jacob, and Jacob was the crooked one. It is *God* who made him Israel, a prince with God. And God wants to do that for the *sons* of Jacob.

Abraham is called the "friend" of God, and God wants to bring these people into a right relationship with Himself.

> **Fear thou not; for I am with thee: be not dismayed; for I am thy God: I will strengthen thee; yea, I will help thee; yea, I will uphold thee with the right hand of my righteousness [Isa. 41:10].**

This verse has been a real pillar of strength and a source of comfort to God's children of every age.

As he moves on, he says that if they oppose God it will be the very height of folly because they are moving toward the day when all these adjustments will have to be made.

Now note this remarkable verse:

> **For I the Lord thy God will hold thy right hand, saying unto thee, Fear not; I will help thee [Isa. 41:13].**

Here is God's gracious overture to trust Him—what comfort! God wants to take us into His confidence. He wants to enable us to walk with Him, have fellowship with Him, and know Him. My, what mankind is missing today! Some people can even get so involved in church work that they miss all this.

> **Fear not, thou worm Jacob, and ye men of Israel; I will help thee, saith the Lord, and thy redeemer, the Holy One of Israel [Isa. 41:14].**

You may think you are something, but you are a "worm"—a nobody. It is only God who can make any of us important. Only God can make man a somebody. Little man frets and struts across the stage of life, as Shakespeare put it. He huffs and puffs like the old wolf around the little pigs' houses. Where is man going, and exactly what is he getting out of what he is doing? Some people see the futility of it all and take their own lives. Where else can they turn? The only place man can turn is to God. Oh, what man is missing! God's fellowship, His salvation, His goodness, His grace—all of these are yours if you but turn to Him.

Then He talks to them about the material blessings of the Millennium—they will be there. And God would like to talk to you and me about the spiritual blessings which are available to us now and those we will have in eternity.

GOD OVERTURNS IDOLS

Produce your cause, saith the Lord; bring forth your strong reasons, saith the King of Jacob [Isa. 41:21].

This is a challenge to idolatry. Now who is an idolater? Have you ever considered the possibility that you may be? Anything you put between your soul and God is your idol—regardless of what it is. It is anything to which you are giving your time and your energy; it could actually be your religion. Anything that you allow to take the place of a personal relationship with God is your idol.

What can idols do? Can they explain the origin of the universe? Are you satisfied today with the explanations that evolution has given? Of course there have been several explanations, but God says, "Bring them all out."

Let them bring forth, and shew us what shall happen: let them shew the former things, what they be, that we may consider them, and know the latter end of them; or declare us things for to come [Isa. 41:22].

Man doesn't know his beginning or the origin of the universe. He simply doesn't know—I don't care what theory he is following. I predict that the evolutionist will be embarrassed in the next fifty years or so because evolution will be just one of the many theories which will be left along the highway of time with the other wreckage. There have been many explanations of the origin of the universe which were called scientific at one time but are exploded today. Evolution will be exploded in time. Then man will turn to another theory. Man doesn't know his origin, and he doesn't know the future. Man is a very ignorant creature. Have you ever stopped to think how little you know?

There are many Ph.D.'s who don't know very much either. I heard of a man working on his Ph.D. who was studying the eye of the mosquito. Now there is an unusual subject! One day as he was doing his research, it suddenly occurred to him that he did not want to spend the rest of his life looking a mosquito in the eye. And I can understand that—I wouldn't mind taking one or two looks, but after that I think it would become monotonous! This man came to the conclusion that he should do something else. He found the Lord Jesus Christ as his Savior, was granted his degree, and he decided to dedicate his life to something worthwhile. Today he is a minister of the gospel.

It is quite interesting that man can be very well-educated, even have his doctor's degree, and still know very little. He knows nothing about his origin or where he is going, and no idol can give him that information. So it is well to turn to the One who does have the answers. This doesn't mean He will give you all the answers, but it is nice to know *Him* who knows the answers. I have never learned much about science, but I did learn a motto that was posted in the science building of the college I attended, which read: "Next to knowing is knowing where to find out." Now there are many things I don't know, but I know the One who knows everything. If there is something I *need* to know, God will tell me.

Behold, ye are of nothing, and your work of nought: an abomination is he that chooseth you [Isa. 41:24].

Man cannot explain his past, and he does not know his future apart from God. That makes all of man's effort apart from God a very vain thing, an empty thing. During my first pastorate a man came to me and said, "If you can't give me a good reason for living, I am going to solve all of my problems by taking my life." What do you do with a man like that? He had an old, rusty .45; it was a big old gun. I said to him, "Now look, if you can show me you can solve your problems by taking your life, I will get you a better gun than the one you have so you can do it right. Candidly, if you are not going to turn to Christ—if

you are not going to bring Him into your life—you might as well use
your gun. I see no reason why you shouldn't." Well, he was really
taken aback. He expected me to give him arguments on reasons for
living. That fellow put down his gun and left. Although he didn't
turn to Christ at that time, he did later on. And he found that Christ
had the answer to his problems.

**Behold, they are all vanity; their works are nothing:
their molten images are wind and confusion [Isa.
41:29].**

"Confusion" is the end result of idolatry or any philosophy which is
anti-God or atheistic. It does not have the answers to the problems of
life. These man-made systems cannot satisfy the human heart. The
answer is found in the One who brings good tidings of great joy.

CHAPTER 42

THEME: The Servant of Jehovah—Jesus; the scourge of idolatry—images; the servant of Jehovah—the nation

In each chapter Isaiah is gradually working up to his condemnation of idolatry.

We find in this chapter that the nation Israel is called the servant of Jehovah. Also, the Lord Jesus Christ is the Servant of Jehovah and is so called in the Gospel of Mark. He made it very clear: "For even the Son of man came not to be ministered unto, but to minister, and to give his life a ransom for many" (Mark 10:45). And in Matthew 12:17–21 there is an application of this prophecy to the Lord Jesus.

THE SERVANT OF JEHOVAH—JESUS

Behold my servant, whom I uphold; mine elect, in whom my soul delighteth; I have put my spirit upon him: he shall bring forth judgment to the Gentiles [Isa. 42:1].

"Behold" is a word that is a bugle call to consider the Lord Jesus Christ.

A bruised reed shall he not break, and the smoking flax shall he not quench: he shall bring forth judgment unto truth [Isa. 42:3].

This verse characterizes the life and ministry of the Lord Jesus when He was here. "A bruised reed shall he not break." The Lord didn't move in with a club against sin. He simply let sin bring its own judgment. "The smoking flax shall he not quench"—the man who keeps on in sin will find that it will break out in flames finally. The wages of sin is death; it always is that. You can't change it.

This is a marvelous section as it presents the Lord Jesus as God's Servant.

> I the LORD called thee in righteousness, and will hold thine hand, and will keep thee, and give thee for a covenant of the people, for a light of the Gentiles;
>
> To open the blind eyes, to bring out the prisoners from the prison, and them that sit in darkness out of the prison house [Isa. 42:6-7].

Christ performed these miracles as credentials of His Kingship when He was here the first time. He came as the Light of the world. As old Simeon prophesied, "A light to lighten the Gentiles, and the glory of thy people Israel" (Luke 2:32).

THE SCOURGE OF IDOLATRY—IMAGES

Now Isaiah begins God's polemic against idolatry.

> I am the LORD: that is my name: and my glory will I not give to another, neither my praise to graven images [Isa. 42:8].

God will not share His glory with another.

Now he talks about the scourge of idolatry, and the judgment of God which it will bring.

> I will make waste mountains and hills, and dry up all their herbs; and I will make the rivers islands, and I will dry up the pools [Isa. 42:15].

The physical earth will be affected by His judgment.

> And I will bring the blind by a way that they knew not; I will lead them in paths that they have not known: I will

make darkness light before them, and crooked things straight. These things will I do unto them, and not forsake them [Isa. 42:16].

This is the way God leads His own. You and I are blind to the future, but He is not, and He will lead all who put their trust in Him.

They shall be turned back, they shall be greatly ashamed, that trust in graven images, that say to the molten images, Ye are our gods [Isa. 42:17].

The idolaters, you see, are warned that judgment is coming.

THE SERVANT OF JEHOVAH—THE NATION

Who is blind, but my servant? or deaf, as my messenger that I sent? who is blind as he that is perfect, and blind as the LORD's servant? [Isa. 42:19].

He identifies the blind servant here as His own people Israel. This is God's condemnation of His own people—

But this is a people robbed and spoiled; they are all of them snared in holes, and they are hid in prison houses: they are for a prey, and none delivereth; for a spoil, and none saith, Restore [Isa. 42:22].

The nation Israel is the subject in this verse. They are "a people robbed and spoiled." Why? Because they turned away from God, and they have turned to idols.

Who gave Jacob for a spoil, and Israel to the robbers? did not the LORD, he against whom we have sinned? for they would not walk in his ways, neither were they obedient unto his law [Isa. 42:24].

The people and nation are identified as Israel. God scattered them—
but He will also regather them.

> **Therefore he hath poured upon him the fury of his an-
> ger, and the strength of battle: and it hath set him on fire
> round about, yet he knew not; and it burned him, yet he
> laid it not to heart [Isa. 42:25].**

The chastening of the Lord did not cause the nation to repent and
return to Him. Did this thwart the purposes of God? The answer, of
course is *no*, as we will see in the following chapter.

CHAPTERS 43 AND 44

THEME: Retrospect—creation, redemption, preserva-
tion of Israel; Prospect—future judgment, deliverance,
redemption of Israel; promise of the Spirit; polemic
against idolatry; prophecy concerning Cyrus

This section of Scripture, particularly chapter 43, reveals that God is not through with the nation Israel. It is tantamount to unbelief to deny that God has a future purpose for the nation of Israel. In the New Testament Paul asks the question, ". . . Hath God cast away His people?" And the answer is, "God forbid . . ." (Rom. 11:1). That is a very dogmatic answer. God is not through with these folk, as He makes clear in the chapter before us.

RETROSPECT—CREATION, REDEMPTION, PRESERVATION OF ISRAEL

But now thus saith the LORD that created thee, O Jacob, and he that formed thee, O Israel, Fear not: for I have redeemed thee, I have called thee by thy name; thou art mine [Isa. 43:1].

This statement is as clear-cut as it could be. God addresses the nation *Israel* in this entire section, and I do not think you could misunderstand Him unless you deliberately wanted to misunderstand.

He speaks of their origin: "the LORD that *created* thee." God took a sad specimen like old Jacob, whose name means "crooked"—he was a supplanter—and made a nation out of him.

God took the dust of the ground, breathed into it the spirit of life, and it became a living human being. And that human being rebelled, but now God makes sons of God out of those who will trust Christ. That is my beginning, and it was a very bad beginning. I don't accept the evolutionary theory that I evolved from a monkey; I came from something worse than a monkey! I came from a rebellious sinner who on the physical side had been taken from the ground. That first man passed on to me a fallen nature which will never be reformed or repaired. But God has given me a new nature.

Beginning with Jacob, God created a nation. Then He *redeemed* them from Egypt by blood and power, and they became Israel, a prince with God. They belong to God because of creation and because of redemption.

> **When thou passest through the waters, I will be with thee; and through the rivers, they shall not overflow thee: when thou walkest through the fire, thou shalt not be burned; neither shall the flame kindle upon thee [Isa. 43:2].**

This is a promise which specifically applies to Israel and the manner in which God delivered them in the past, for example, when they crossed the Red Sea and the Jordan River.

It also has a marvelous spiritual application for all of God's children in all times. "When thou passest through the waters, I will be with thee." Sometimes in my experience I get into what I could call "deep water" when I can't touch bottom. But I have the assurance that God is going through the experience with me. I think I'm going to drown, but He has promised, "they shall not overflow thee," and He intervenes and delivers me.

> **For I am the LORD thy God, the Holy One of Israel, thy Saviour: I gave Egypt for thy ransom, Ethiopia and Seba for thee [Isa. 43:3].**

He does not lower His high standard in salvation. How could God give Egypt and Ethiopia ransom for Israel? The answer is simple. God says in effect, "I used these nations to discipline you. I *gave* them, that is, I *permitted* them to treat you as they did, and now I will judge them."

In Proverbs 21:18 we read, "The wicked shall be a ransom for the righteous, and the transgressor for the upright." Have you ever wondered why God permitted the enemy to cross your path and cause you all the trouble he did? He did it in order to bring you into line and in order to develop you spiritually. God gave him for your deliverance. Proverbs 11:8 says, "The righteous is delivered out of trouble, and the wicked cometh in his stead." God has let several people really mistreat me, and I talked to Him about it. I thought God was treating me wrong, but I noticed that the Lord paddled these individuals, and I must confess that I was rather satisfied about it. The Lord used these people to straighten things out in my life, and then He straightened them out.

> **Since thou wast precious in my sight, thou hast been honourable, and I have loved thee: therefore will I give men for thee, and people for thy life [Isa. 43:4].**

We cannot imagine how much God loves Israel. We cannot imagine how precious we are to God.

> **Fear not: for I am with thee: I will bring thy seed from the east, and gather thee from the west;**
>
> **I will say to the north, Give up; and to the south, Keep not back: bring my sons from far, and my daughters from the ends of the earth [Isa. 43:5–6].**

God states in clear-cut language that He will regather the nation Israel. In Jeremiah 31:10 He reaffirms this: "Hear the word of the LORD, O ye nations, and declare it in the isles afar off, and say, He that scattered Israel will gather him, and keep him, as a shepherd doth his flock." God says, "Hear the word of the LORD, O ye nations." What He means is this: "Hear the word of the Lord, ye liberals. Hear the word of the Lord, ye amillennialists, and ye postmillennialists, and ye premillennialists—some of you haven't been quite sure whether or not I am through with Israel." We are to listen to Him. Regardless of what the world situation might be, God says He intends to regather Israel. We have His word for it.

> Ye are my witnesses, saith the LORD, and my servant
> whom I have chosen: that ye may know and believe me,
> and understand that I am he: before me there was no
> God formed, neither shall there be after me [Isa. 43:10].

God has no competitor or equal. He alone is God. He alone holds this unique position.

> I, even I, am the LORD; and beside me there is no saviour
> [Isa. 43:11].

It is interesting that of all the religions of the world only Christianity guarantees salvation. Others put down quite a program, but they certainly do not guarantee salvation. God says, "Beside me there is no saviour."

God now opens up the subject of idolatry.

> I have declared, and have saved, and I have shewed,
> when there was no strange god among you: therefore ye
> are my witnesses, saith the LORD, that I am God [Isa.
> 43:12].

God is saying, "As long as you will not go into idolatry or turn to that which will lead you away from Me, I will bless you."

PROSPECT—FUTURE JUDGMENT, DELIVERANCE, REDEMPTION OF ISRAEL

> Yea, before the day was I am he; and there is none that
> can deliver out of my hand: I will work, and who shall
> let it? [Isa. 43:13].

The word *let* in this verse means to hinder. No creature can slip out of the hand of God or escape out of His reach.

> Thus saith the LORD, your redeemer, the Holy One of Israel; For your sake I have sent to Babylon, and have brought down all their nobles, and the Chaldeans, whose cry is in the ships [Isa. 43:14].

The ultimate destruction of Babylon is foretold.

> I am the LORD, your Holy One, the creator of Israel, your King [Isa. 43:15].

Surely it is inescapable that the nation Israel is the subject. God takes responsibility for bringing them into existence. Let every anti-Semite take note of this. He is their King. This is another affirmation of the deity of Christ, for He is their King. When the Lord Jesus came to earth and made His claim to Kingship, Israel knew that He was claiming to be Immanuel, ". . . God with us" (Matt. 1:23). The instructed Israelite understood that.

We have seen that God claims Israel because He created them. Now He speaks of the fact that even the beasts of the field honor Him.

> The beast of the field shall honour me, the dragons and the owls: because I give waters in the wilderness and rivers in the desert, to give drink to my people, my chosen [Isa. 43:20].

I have a notion that even the animal world is a little more conscious of God than His creature man, who has fallen into sin.

> I, even I, am he that blotteth out thy transgressions for mine own sake, and will not remember thy sins [Isa. 43:25].

God is saying that He intends to forgive them on the same basis that He has forgiven us.

Thy first father hath sinned, and thy teachers have transgressed against me [Isa. 43:27].

This evidently is a reference to Abraham. Surely Scripture records his failures and sins. We have only to mention the matter of his lying to Pharaoh about Sarah, his wife.

Thy teachers means "interpreters." Those who interpreted God to the people had faults and sins. Remember Samson, Samuel, and David.

Therefore I have profaned the princes of the sanctuary, and have given Jacob to the curse, and Israel to reproaches [Isa. 43:28].

This is the present condition of Israel. They have no peace today because they have departed from the living and true God.

This is not, however, their final state.

Chapter 44 continues the theme of chapter 43. However, the last chapter closes with the dark mention of coming judgment. This chapter moves into the light of the coming Kingdom and the promise of the Holy Spirit.

There is in this chapter a brilliant and bitterly devastating satire against idolatry. This is the recurring theme of this particular section. The human heart has a way of turning from God to some idol. Today, we do not go after graven images, but anything to which a person gives himself instead of the true God is an idol. It can be a career, the making of money, seeking for fame, pleasure, sex, alcohol, self-adoration, or business. These are our idols, O America! The high point of the prophet's polemic against idolatry will come in chapter 46. There we shall have occasion to consider this subject further and to examine the real distinction between God and an idol.

PROMISE OF THE SPIRIT

God calls to Israel as His chosen one and assures her of His help. Then there is this remarkable prophecy of the Holy Spirit:

**For I will pour water upon him that is thirsty, and floods
upon the dry ground: I will pour my spirit upon thy
seed, and my blessing upon thine offspring [Isa. 44:3].**

This, I believe, is a reference to the pouring out of the Spirit, which
corresponds to Joel 2:28–32. If you read Joel's prophecy very carefully,
you will find that it was not fulfilled on the Day of Pentecost. When
Peter quoted from it, he did two things. First, he said, "this is that"—
he did not say it was a fulfillment (see Acts 2:16). The crowd there in
Jerusalem was ridiculing the disciples because they were speaking in
different languages of the ". . . wonderful works of God" (Acts 2:11).
The people were accusing them of being ". . . full of new wine" (Acts
2:13), instead of the Holy Spirit. So Peter says in substance, "This
should not amaze you, because this is similar to what will take place
in the last days." Now how do we know it wasn't fulfilled on the Day
of Pentecost? There are several reasons: (1) Joel said, "And I will shew
wonders in the heavens and in the earth, blood, and fire, and pillars of
smoke. The sun shall be turned into darkness, and the moon into
blood . . ." (Joel 2:30–31). This did not take place on the Day of Pentecost. (2) The record in Acts tells us that the Spirit was not poured out
on all people, but Joel said: ". . . I will pour out my spirit upon all
flesh . . ." (Joel 2:28). In Acts there were first 120 disciples, then 3,000
believers—not ever "all," and after nineteen hundred years it still is
not *all*. There were probably a half million to a million people in Jerusalem at that time, but by no stretch of the imagination can anyone say
that Joel's prophecy was fulfilled at that time. But the fulfillment of
Joel's prophecy is coming in the future. This is the reason I continually say that the greatest days for God are in the future.

POLEMIC AGAINST IDOLATRY

In verses 9–20 we have a brilliant polemic against idolatry. The way
the prophet deals with the subject is devastating. Those who make
images are witnesses to the senseless character of their gods. An
image does not even have the five senses of a human being. An idol

can't hear, see, talk, smell, or feel. Paul called them "nothings," and that is what they are. They cannot help anyone.

> **Who hath formed a god, or molten a graven image that is profitable for nothing? [Isa. 44:10].**

The prophet asks the question, "Why do you spend all of your time making a god? You ought to be ashamed. You have everything mixed up. You don't make a god; *God* made you!"

Now he goes on to describe idol making—

> **The smith with the tongs both worketh in the coals, and fashioneth it with hammers, and worketh it with the strength of his arms: yea, he is hungry, and his strength faileth: he drinketh no water, and is faint [Isa. 44:12].**

The artificer of metals works hard in forging a god from some metal, but this labor weakens him and reveals that he is but a man. After all of his labor, talent, time, and money that he puts into making a god, what does he get? Nothing! He gets a beautiful little "nothing."

The origin of a man-made god begins in a forest; yet it is God who made the tree to begin with! Only God can make a tree.

> **Then shall it be for a man to burn: for he will take thereof, and warm himself; yea, he kindleth it, and baketh bread; yea, he maketh a god, and worshippeth it; he maketh it a graven image, and falleth down thereto [Isa. 44:15].**

The chips and scraps from the production of a god are used to kindle a fire for the man to warm himself and to bake bread. This is the only practical and helpful contribution that comes from the making of a god. In fact, the scraps are helpful, but that idol is no good to you at all. It cannot warm you; it cannot cook your food; it cannot help you; it cannot save you. An idol cannot do anything for you. God is calling Israel's attention to how absurd idolatry really is.

My friend, many of us give ourselves to those things that take us away from God. They don't help us, they don't lift us up, they don't bring us joy, and it is a fact that they can never save us.

PROPHECY CONCERNING CYRUS

That saith of Cyrus, He is my shepherd, and shall perform all my pleasure: even saying to Jerusalem, Thou shalt be built; and to the temple, Thy foundation shall be laid [Isa. 44:28].

Keep in mind that this verse really belongs in the next chapter. This is a remarkable prophecy concerning Cyrus. He is named here about two centuries before his birth. He is designated as "my shepherd." This is the only instance where a pagan potentate is given such a title. We shall develop this in the next chapter.

CHAPTER 45

THEME: Calling of Cyrus before he was born; creation of the universe; continuance of Israel

This chapter continues the theme of the preceding chapter. This chapter begins with Cyrus as the last chapter closed with him. It is rather unfortunate that the final verse of chapter 44 is not the first verse of this chapter, but I am sure you understand that chapter and verse divisions were made of men. It is said that a monk of the Middle Ages marked off the chapters while riding a donkey through the Alps. Each time the donkey came to a halt, he came forward with his pen, and that marked the end of a chapter. Of course, this is a fable, but it looks as if certain places were certainly divided that way. In fact, there are times when I get the impression that perhaps the donkey did some dividing on his own!

Let me repeat the final verse of chapter 44, since it properly belongs here:

> **That saith of Cyrus, He is my shepherd, and shall perform all my pleasure: even saying to Jerusalem, Thou shalt be built; and to the temple, Thy foundation shall be laid [Isa. 44:28].**

Cyrus was named and identified almost two hundred years before he was born. This unusual prophecy has caused the liberal critic to construct out of the web of his imagination the figment of "the great unknown" writer of this section of the Book of Isaiah. The fact that Isaiah could name a man two centuries before he appears is too strong a tonic for the weak faith of an unbeliever.

The question is, "Why was Cyrus marked out like this two centuries before he was born?" I believe there are three reasons. Primarily it was for identification. When Cyrus did appear on the scene, there would be no misunderstanding about whom Isaiah had spoken. Also,

Cyrus would be the man responsible for a decree that would return the nation Israel to her land.

Another reason Isaiah called Cyrus by name through the revelation of God was so that his accuracy could be demonstrated. If in two hundred years Isaiah would be accurate about Cyrus, he also would be accurate in his prophecy concerning the One born of a virgin, Immanuel, God with us, who was to come seven hundred years later. The instructed Israelite should have been prepared for Christ's coming.

Notice that God calls Cyrus "my shepherd," and says that he "shall perform all my pleasure" and shall rebuild Jerusalem.

Remember that God used Assyria to take the northern kingdom of Israel into captivity. Then He used Babylon to destroy Jerusalem and take the southern kingdom into captivity. The men God used to do this were wicked, and God judged them for what they had done. But Cyrus is different. God calls him "my shepherd" who shall "perform all my pleasure."

When we get to heaven I believe there will be two things that will be a surprise to all of us: (1) the folk who will be there whom we didn't expect to make it—and I think Cyrus is going to be one of them, and (2) the folk whom we expected to be there who won't be there. And, my friend, the only reason any of us will be there is because Christ is our Savior.

It is interesting to note that God says that Cyrus "shall perform all my *pleasure*"—not only God's *will*, but also His *pleasure*. After all, both Sennacherib and Nebuchadnezzar performed God's *will* in taking Israel and Judah into captivity, but Cyrus will perform God's *pleasure*, and that is a little different.

CALLING OF CYRUS BEFORE HE WAS BORN

Thus saith the LORD to his anointed, to Cyrus, whose right hand I have holden, to subdue nations before him; and I will loose the loins of kings, to open before him the two leaved gates; and the gates shall not be shut [Isa. 45:1].

This is a remarkable prophecy. Cyrus did not appear in the pages of history until two hundred years after Isaiah spoke of him. Cyrus came out of the East, from Persia. The ruins of his tomb have been found in Pasargadae, Iran, and you cannot read the inscription without recognizing that he was a humble man who trusted God. Most of the great rulers of the past were braggarts and most of them were liars. Everything they said you have to take with a grain of salt. The records they left magnified their greatness (sort of like the ones left by modern politicians) and cannot be trusted. But Cyrus was different. He made no great claims; he did not boast, and yet, he conquered the world!

Also note that God calls Cyrus "his anointed," a title that applies only to the Lord Jesus. Why did God give such a title to Cyrus? Because he carried out the will of God and delivered the Israelites from captivity and permitted them to return to the Land of Promise. Also he encouraged the Israelites who did not return to send rich gifts of gold, silver, and precious things with those who did go back. In that respect Cyrus was a gentile messiah of Israel and a vague foreshadowing of the One who was to come.

"The two leaved gates" is evidently a reference to the numerous gates of Babylon which shut Israel out from returning to Palestine. Cyrus opened those gates and said that the Israelites could walk out. They were free to return to their homeland.

Now God says this of Cyrus:

> **And I will give thee the treasures of darkness, and hidden riches of secret places, that thou mayest know that I, the LORD, which call thee by thy name, am the God of Israel [Isa. 45:3].**

The rich treasures of Babylon, which the kings of Babylon had taken as spoils of war from all nations, especially from Jerusalem, fell to Cyrus.

> **For Jacob my servant's sake, and Israel mine elect, I have even called thee by thy name: I have surnamed thee, though thou hast not known me.**

> **I am the LORD, and there is none else, there is no God beside me: I girded thee, though thou hast not known me [Isa. 45:4–5].**

God chose Cyrus before he knew the Lord. It is reasonable to conclude that Cyrus came to know the living and true God. "Thus saith Cyrus king of Persia, The LORD God of heaven hath given me all the kingdoms of the earth; and he hath charged me to build him an house at Jerusalem, which is in Judah" (Ezra 1:2).

CREATION OF THE UNIVERSE

Here is a remarkable statement relative to the creation of the universe before all time.
   God says:

> **I form the light, and create darkness: I make peace, and create evil, I the LORD do all these things [Isa. 45:7].**

Zoroastrianism began in Persia. It teaches that Mazda is the god of light. God says He creates light, and that it is no god. The Persians were getting very close to the truth. Many have wondered why they worshiped one god in the midst of idolatry. Well, you must remember that they came in contact with the nation Israel, and Israel was a witness to the world. In Zoroastrianism darkness was Ahriman, the god of evil. God takes responsibility for creating the darkness also.
   "And create evil"—the word *evil* does not mean wickedness in this instance, but rather "sorrow, difficulties, or tragedies"—those things which are the fruit of evil, the fruit of sin. This is the Old Testament way of saying, "The wages of sin is death . . ." (Rom. 6:23). If you indulge in sin, there will be a payday for it!
   By the way, let me introduce something else at this point, since we are living in a day when it is said that good and evil are relative terms, that whatever you *think* is good, *is* good. The argument is put forth: The Bible says "Thou shalt not kill" and "Thou shalt not steal" (Exod. 20:13, 15). But what is the Bible? Who should obey it? Or why should we listen to the God of the Bible?

The Lord has another very cogent argument. God says that if you indulge in sin, you will find that sin has its payday. It pays a full wage, by the way. This is what God is saying through Isaiah. God has so created the universe that when you break over the bounds that He has set, you don't need a judge, a hangman's noose, or an electric chair; God will take care of it.

He says, therefore, that He is the One who creates light and darkness. He is answering Zoroastrianism which worshiped the god of light. God says, "I want you to know that light is no god; I created it."

Woe unto him that striveth with his Maker! Let the potsherd strive with the potsherds of the earth. Shall the clay say to him that fashioneth it, What makest thou? or thy work, He hath no hands? [Isa. 45:9].

Why fight against God? You are going to lose anyway. The Greeks had a proverb that went something like this: The dice of the gods are loaded. That is exactly what God says in His Word. He says, "Don't think that you can fight Me. Settle your case out of court." "Come now, and let us reason together, saith the LORD: though your sins be as scarlet, they shall be as white as snow; though they be red like crimson, they shall be as wool" (Isa. 1:18).

My friend, don't gamble with God, because when He rolls the dice He knows exactly how they are coming up—you don't. This is tremendous!

Now the Lord makes some other claims.

I have made the earth, and created man upon it: I, even my hands, have stretched out the heavens, and all their host have I commanded [Isa. 45:12].

It is interesting that God says He "stretched out the heavens." This is no accident. It was Sir James Jeans, a Christian astronomer in Great Britain, who advanced a theory that today most astronomers follow. I notice here in Pasadena that some of the men connected with Cal

Tech, who work in the field of astronomy, take the position that you and I live in a universe which Sir James Jeans called an expanding universe. It gets bigger every minute. The planets and worlds and galactic systems are all moving out away from each other. God says, "I stretched out the heavens." That is the way He did it although He hasn't told us exactly *how* He did it—or how He could take nothing and make something out of it. Regardless of what theory you adopt, you have to move back to the place where there is *nothing* and then there is *something*. If you can tell me how nothing becomes something, then I will listen to you. Until you can answer that, you can talk about tadpoles and monkeys all you want and I'll just sit and smile at you. I'm a skeptic; I don't believe you. Only God has a reasonable answer. God says, "I created it." By His fiat word He brought the universe into existence. Do you have a more intelligent answer than what God has given to us in His Word?

CONTINUANCE OF ISRAEL

This brings us to the third division: the continuance of Israel for all time and eternity. God won't let us forget this subject.

> **But Israel shall be saved in the Lord with an everlasting salvation: ye shall not be ashamed nor confounded world without end [Isa. 45:17].**

Those who believe that God is through with Israel should take a long look at this passage. Israel's salvation is everlasting. God says, "Yes, you are going to be judged, Israel. You are going to Babylon, but you are going to return to the land. Rebellion is still in your heart, but ultimately I am going to save you."

Again He gives them an invitation—it was wide open then and it is wide open today.

> **Look unto me, and be ye saved, all the ends of the earth: for I am God, and there is none else [Isa. 45:22].**

This is the verse, used by an ignorant man, which was responsible for the conversion of Charles Spurgeon. Spurgeon was on his way to church one Sunday morning when a snowstorm hit London. Because he couldn't make it to his church, he stopped at a little church along the way. The storm was so severe that the preacher did not make it to this little church, so a man got up and said a few words. Spurgeon never knew the man's name; he only knew that he was an uneducated man. He chose Isaiah 45:22 as his text, and what he lacked in lightning, he made up for in thunder. He said, "This verse says, 'Look unto me, and be ye saved.'" He began to talk about the verse. "God says you should *look* to Him and be *saved*." By that time he ran out of ammunition. He had said all he could say about the verse, so he went into the thunder department and began to roar and pound the pulpit, "Look to God, all the ends of the earth, and be saved." He looked way back in the congregation and saw the young fellow Spurgeon sitting there with a very miserable look on his face. The man said to Spurgeon, "You look to Jesus, and you will be saved." Spurgeon was a very brilliant man, but he did what this ignorant man suggested—he looked to Jesus and was saved.

CHAPTER 46

THEME: Pronouncement of judgment against idols

This chapter contains one of the finest satires against idolatry that is found in the Word of God. It opens with the announcement of defeat against the idols of Babylon in particular. This seems strange since Babylon had not yet come to the front as a world power and was not the enemy of Israel. Nevertheless, Babylon was the source of all idolatry, and it is fitting that after announcing the defeat of the idols of Babylon the prophet proceeds to denounce all idolatry with an injunction to Israel not to forsake the true God.

PRONOUNCEMENT OF JUDGMENT AGAINST IDOLS

Bel boweth down, Nebo stoopeth, their idols were upon the beasts, and upon the cattle: your carriages were heavy loaden; they are a burden to the weary beast [Isa. 46:1].

Bel and Nebo are gods of Babylon. *Bel* is the shortened form of Baal and is found in the first part of Beelzebub—which is one of Satan's names. Nebo means "speaker or prophet." When Paul and Barnabas went to Lystra, the people thought Barnabas was Bel or Jupiter and Paul was Nebo or Mercury because he did the talking.

Behind the idols of that day was satanic worship, which is becoming rather popular in our contemporary society. The Word of God repeatedly warns us that our warfare is *spiritual* warfare.

God contrasts the helplessness of the idol, which is a burden to carry, to His own love and strength.

Hearken unto me, O house of Jacob, and all the remnant of the house of Israel, which are borne by me from the belly, which are carried from the womb [Isa. 46:3].

God says, "I have been carrying you, Israel, as a woman carries a child in her womb."

> **And even to your old age I am he; and even to hoar hairs will I carry you: I have made, and I will bear; even I will carry, and will deliver [Isa. 46:4].**

This is the real distinction between that which is true and that which is false. God had not only been carrying the nation Israel, but He had carried each individual from the cradle to the grave. Let me ask you the question, "Is your religion carrying you, or are you carrying your religion?" God carries our sins. "He hath borne our griefs, and carried our sorrows" (Isa. 53:4). He also carries our cares, our burdens: "Casting all your care upon him; for he careth for you" (1 Pet. 5:7). And God carries us today: "The eternal God is thy refuge, and underneath are the everlasting arms: and he shall thrust out the enemy from before thee; and shall say, Destroy them" (Deut. 33:27).

Now notice how He speaks of idolatry:

> **To whom will ye liken me, and make me equal, and compare me, that we may be like? [Isa. 46:5].**

The reason that it is so difficult to explain God is because He is infinite and we are finite and live in a finite universe. There is nothing with which to compare Him. He cannot be reduced to our terminology without losing all meaning. He cannot be translated into human language. This explains one of the reasons why God became a man. The only way we can know God is through Jesus. He revealed God.

This is a brilliant satire on idolatry—

> **They lavish gold out of the bag, and weigh silver in the balance, and hire a goldsmith; and he maketh it a god: they fall down, yea, they worship [Isa. 46:6].**

This is a metallic image that excels the wooden image in beauty and value. The wealth of man is expended in making an idol. If a man doesn't have much money, he has a cheap god. If he is rich, he has a rich god. It actually amounts to men worshiping their own workmanship, which is self-worship. It is a form of humanism.

Now here is the real test:

> **They bear him upon the shoulder, they carry him, and set him in his place, and he standeth; from his place shall he not remove: yea, one shall cry unto him, yet can he not answer, nor save him out of his trouble [Isa. 46:7].**

They lug their god around on their shoulders and put him in the corner when they get home! Listen to what God says to them—

> **Remember the former things of old: for I am God, and there is none else; I am God, and there is none like me [Isa. 46:9].**

There is a lot of modern idolatry about. Face up to it. Do you receive anything when you go to church? For many folk church-going is a real burden to them. It is like a useless god they have to carry around.

Oh, my friend, God wants to communicate to you. He has something for you. He doesn't want you to carry Him; He wants to carry you.

CHAPTER 47

THEME: The decline and fall of Babylon

This is the third time in this book (chs. 13—14; 21) that we have considered the prediction of the doom of Babylon. There was also a suggestion of the fall of Babylon in chapter 46, which opened with God's judgment upon the idols. The time given to this subject is remarkable in view of the fact that Babylon at this time was a very small and insignificant kingdom. It was almost a century before it would become a world power. It had been in existence since the days of the Tower of Babel and had influenced the world religiously. Babylon was the fountainhead and the mother of all idolatry. Again I recommend for your study Alexander Hislop's book, *The Two Babylons*. All through the Old Testament books of prophecy a great deal is said about drunkenness and idolatry. These are the two things that will bring the downfall of any nation.

There is a spiritual meaning for us of the present who have nothing to do with Babylon of the past or of the future. The Babylon of the past lies under the rubble and ruin of judgment. Its glory is diminished by the accumulated dust of the centuries. We can see this Babylonian tendency today in the political realm as represented in the United Nations. Babel is the place where all the political power of the world comes together, which will finally be under the willful king, the Antichrist. We see the commercial combine coming to pass in the breaking down of economic barriers among the nations of Europe. We see the religious combine in both Romanism and the World Council of Churches. We will see all of this prefigured in ancient Babylon.

DECLINE OF BABYLON

Come down, and sit in the dust, O virgin daughter of Babylon, sit on the ground: there is no throne, O daugh-

ter of the Chaldeans: for thou shalt no more be called
tender and delicate [Isa. 47:1].

"Come down" is the command of God to Babylon, the same as a dog
is called to obedience. It is like saying, "Down Rover, down Fido."
That is the way God is going to talk to the great world power Babylon
when the time comes for it to be brought low. God will say, "Down
Fido, down Babylon." That is the way the Lord Jesus dealt with the
storm on the little sea of Galilee. When the Lord spoke to the waves
and the wind, He literally said, "Be muzzled," like you would muzzle
a dog. The same thought is here in Isaiah.

Babylon is called a virgin because she had not yet been captured
by an enemy. Babylon was just now coming to power although it had
a very ancient history, going back to Nimrod (see Gen. 10) and to Babel where the Tower of Babel (see Gen. 11) was located. All the ziggu-
rats in that valley were patterned after the Tower of Babel.

He predicts the tremendous humiliation of Babylon—

Take the millstones, and grind meal: uncover thy locks,
make bare the leg, uncover the thigh, pass over the rivers [Isa. 47:2].

This depicts the indescribable humiliation to which Babylon was finally subjected. She had mistreated the people of Israel, and the day
came when she was brought low.

Nudity is becoming rather popular today. Men play with the subject like a child playing with a new toy, but it degrades humanity. It
was no accident that God clothed mankind. A person who wants to go
without clothes has a hangup—a real hangup. For Babylon nudity was
part of her humiliation.

Thy nakedness shall be uncovered, yea, thy shame shall
be seen: I will take vengeance, and I will not meet thee
as a man [Isa. 47:3].

DELIVERANCE OF ISRAEL TO BABYLON

Here we see that God delivered Israel into the hands of Babylon—

> I was wroth with my people, I have polluted mine inher-
> itance, and given them into thine hand: thou didst shew
> them no mercy; upon the ancient hast thou very heavily
> laid thy yoke [Isa. 47:6].

God is making it clear to them that the reason Babylon was able to take His people was because He permitted it and not because Babylon was so superior. They had a great sense of power, and they gave themselves credit for overthrowing Israel. They were wrong. God delivered His people into the hands of Babylon because they had sinned against Him. He was judging His own people. This is the message of the little prophecy of Habakkuk.

> And thou saidst, I shall be a lady for ever: so that thou
> didst not lay these things to thy heart, neither didst re-
> member the latter end of it [Isa. 47:7].

God's judgment of His people deceived Babylon. They thought it was by their might and power that they had taken God's people.

> Therefore hear now this, thou that art given to plea-
> sures, that dwellest carelessly, that sayest in thine
> heart, I am, and none else beside me; I shall not sit as a
> widow, neither shall I know the loss of children [Isa.
> 47:8].

Babylon was arrogant, lifted up, and careless, not believing that a frightful fall was coming. Nebuchadnezzar, the Babylonian king, looked over the beautiful and glorious city of Babylon, and said, "This is great Babylon that I have built," giving no credit to God. God sent him out to the field like an ox to eat grass, having a form of amnesia—probably the psychiatrist would call it hysteria today. For a

long time he did not know who he was, and he lived like an animal. It
was God's judgment upon him.

DETAILS FOR THE DESTRUCTION OF BABYLON

**For thou hast trusted in thy wickedness: thou hast said,
None seeth me. Thy wisdom and thy knowledge, it hath
perverted thee; and thou hast said in thine heart, I am,
and none else beside me [Isa. 47:10].**

There is always a grave danger of a nation or a man being lifted up by
pride and feeling that he is able to make it on his own. We are living in
a country today where men can become rich, not by doing some great
service or by making a contribution to mankind, but by being in an
industry that brings men down—degrades them instead of building
them up. Think of the millions of dollars that are being made through
entertainment and the multitudes who are getting rich through the
sale of liquor. We are in many questionable businesses as a nation,
and our methods of business are not always honorable. We attempt to
cover up these things, but God sees, and He will judge as He judged
Babylon.

DILEMMA OF BABYLON

**Stand now with thine enchantments, and with the multi-
tude of thy sorceries, wherein thou hast laboured from
thy youth; if so be thou shalt be able to profit, if so thou
mayest prevail [Isa. 47:12].**

God satirically urges Babylon to turn to the witchcraft in which she
has trusted and which has gotten her into trouble. In substance God
asks, "You thought it was so great, why don't you trust it to get you out
of trouble?"

**Thou art wearied in the multitude of thy counsels. Let
now the astrologers, the stargazers, the monthly prog-**

nosticators, stand up, and save thee from these things that shall come upon thee [Isa. 47:13].

Confusion characterizes Babylon at this time. The city lives up to its name—*Babylon* means "confusion," and confusion besets them. That great city depended upon its economic strength and its total gross product. But something happened to that nation, and it was dying within. We are living in a country today that depends upon its economic strength, but something is also wrong with us, and we won't face up to it. Our problem is moral. As a nation we have departed from the living and true God. The ancient city of Babylon, which at first glance seems so unrelated to us, has a message for us. The stones of the debris of Babylon are crying out a warning to us.

CHAPTER 48

All three of these last sections conclude with the phrase, "no peace . . . to the wicked" (Isa. 57:21). The Messiah brings peace, but those who reject Him will never know peace. Turning to idols is turning from the Messiah. As we have seen, this section has majored in a denunciation of idolatry. Idolatry is a road that leads to Babylon. God, in this book, is traveling the lonely road to Calvary.

LAST CALL TO THE HOUSE OF JACOB

Hear ye this, O house of Jacob, which are called by the name of Israel, and are come forth out of the waters of Judah, which swear by the name of the Lord, and make mention of the God of Israel, but not in truth, nor in righteousness [Isa. 48:1].

There are those who say that Judah and Israel are different, God contradicts that thinking in this verse. Don't try to change the name God has given them. The whole house of Israel is addressed here, and they belong to the chosen line through Abraham, Isaac, and Jacob. The apostate nation back then and in our day should listen to this final injunction to turn back to God. They speak of the God of Israel as though they know Him. Actually, they neither know Him nor serve Him. They have a religion without any strength whatsoever. They will not find the solution to their problems by turning to the United States, or to Russia, or to the Arab nations. Help will come when they turn to God. That is their solution and our solution.

For they call themselves of the holy city, and stay themselves upon the God of Israel; The Lord of hosts is his name [Isa. 48:2].

They boast of being citizens of Jerusalem and of being children of God, but they are such only in name; they are actually strangers to God.

> **Because I knew that thou art obstinate, and thy neck is an iron sinew, and thy brow brass [Isa. 48:4].**

From the very beginning, when God took Israel out of Egypt, He knew they were stiff-necked people. My friend, God did not choose them because they were superior, nor did He choose us because we are superior. God chose them and us because of His grace and because He saw our great need.

LONGING CALL OF GOD TO THE REMNANT

He is pleading with His people to listen to Him.

> **Hearken unto me, O Jacob and Israel, my called; I am he; I am the first, I also am the last [Isa. 48:12].**

It would seem that God is no longer addressing the nation as a whole but confines His word to the remnant labeled, "my called."

> **I, even I, have spoken; yea, I have called him: I have brought him, and he shall make his way prosperous [Isa. 48:15].**

This is the heart cry of God.

> **Come ye near unto me, hear ye this; I have not spoken in secret from the beginning; from the time that it was, there am I: and now the Lord GOD, and his spirit, hath sent me [Isa. 48:16].**

It is Isaiah who becomes God's messenger. He is pleading with them, and as He pleads you can hear the Lord Jesus Christ. F. Delitzsch

(p. 253) appropriately says, "Since the prophet has not spoken in his own person before; whereas, on the other hand, these words are followed in the next chapter by an address concerning Himself from that servant of Jehovah who announces Himself as the restorer of Israel and light of the Gentiles, and who cannot be therefore either Israel, as a nation, or Isaiah, it can be none other than the Lord Jesus Christ Himself."

God has never been able to bless the nation Israel to the fullness of His promise, and you and I have never been blessed as much as God would like to bless us. Whose fault is it? Is it God's fault? No! It is Israel's fault and the fault of you and me.

> **Thy seed also had been as the sand, and the offspring of thy bowels like the gravel thereof; his name should not have been cut off nor destroyed from before me [Isa. 48:19].**

Then he concludes this section, as the three sections of this last major division of Isaiah conclude:

> **There is no peace, saith the LORD, unto the wicked [Isa. 48:22].**

This is the solemn benediction of this section where God's Servant is set over against all the idols of the heathen. He alone gives peace. If a person is away from God, living in sin, he cannot find peace in the world today. We have several thousand years of recorded history which tell us that anyone away from God hasn't had peace.

CHAPTER 49

THEME: Discourse of Christ to the world; discussion of Jehovah with Israel; digression—judgment of Israel's oppressors

In this third and final division of the Book of Isaiah there is a threefold division which is marked off with the words, "There is no peace, saith the LORD, unto the wicked." We have seen in the first division the *comfort* of Jehovah which comes through the servant. Now chapter 49 begins the second division, which I call *salvation* of Jehovah which comes through the suffering Servant.

We are now beginning to move toward a definite revelation of the Lord Jesus Christ as the suffering Servant of God. We have been moving toward that revelation from the very beginning, but at first we saw Him more as a silhouette in the background as the Servant who brings comfort to God's people. The closer we get to chapter 53, where we have that wonderful revelation of the Cross of Christ, the more clear He will become to us.

Israel was the servant of Jehovah, but as such Israel had failed. Now God speaks of another Servant, and that Servant is the Lord Jesus Christ. The prophetic Scriptures spoke primarily of *Israel* as God's servant; yet the final meaning is found in the Person of Christ. A classic illustration is in Hosea 11:1, where it is recorded: "When Israel was a child, then I loved him, and called my son out of Egypt." This was fulfilled in Christ (see Matt. 2:15). The nation failed, but the One who came out of the nation will succeed.

DISCOURSE OF CHRIST TO THE WORLD

As we open this chapter, we are listening in on a discourse by Christ as truly as the twelve apostles listened to Him in Galilee. In this chapter we see Christ moving out to become the Savior of the world. In this movement Israel is not forsaken, for her assured restoration to the land is reaffirmed.

There is nothing to correspond to this remarkable discourse of our Lord Jesus Christ in the religions of this world. Here is One who is looking at a *world*, and He is looking at it as the Servant of God, who has come as the Savior of the world. Every religion is confined to an ethnic group or to several ethnic groups. Generally they do not move beyond the borders of a tribe, a people, or a nation, so that most deities are *local* deities. However, the Deity in the Word of God is the living God, the Creator of the universe and the Redeemer of mankind. This fact makes the discourse before us remarkable indeed.

> **Listen, O isles, unto me; and hearken, ye people, from far; The LORD hath called me from the womb; from the bowels of my mother hath he made mention of my name [Isa. 49:1].**

Christ is calling upon the nations of the world to hear. He was given the name of Jesus before He was born, and this name is to be proclaimed throughout the world because it is the name of the *Savior*, and the world needs a Savior.

> **And he hath made my mouth like a sharp sword; in the shadow of his hand hath he hid me, and made me a polished shaft; in his quiver hath he hid me [Isa. 49:2].**

The sharp sword that went out of His mouth is the Word of God, and the explanation of His enemies when He walked on this earth was, ". . . Never man spake like this man" (John 7:46). And the *revelation* of this One concludes with these words: "And out of his mouth goeth a sharp sword, that with it he should smite the nations . . ." (Rev. 19:15). It is the judgment of the nations by the Word of God.

Notice the identification:

And said unto me, Thou art my servant, O Israel, in whom I will be glorified [Isa. 49:3].

This will be true of the nation Israel, and it is true of Christ. Now this is a remarkable statement:

Then I said, I have laboured in vain, I have spent my strength for nought, and in vain: yet surely my judgment is with the LORD; and my work with my God [Isa. 49:4].

Though the Lord was rejected, and it may look as if He labored in vain, His confidence is in God. Even the *death* of the Lord Jesus Christ was a victory; in fact, it is the greatest victory the world has seen up to the present time. The emphasis in this section, therefore, is on the suffering Servant.

At His first coming He did not gather Israel, as they rejected Him. At His first coming He did something far more wonderful—He wrought salvation for the world. Therefore, God's purposes were not thwarted by man's little machinations.

And now, saith the LORD that formed me from the womb to be his servant, to bring Jacob again to him, Though Israel be not gathered, yet shall I be glorious in the eyes of the LORD, and my God shall be my strength [Isa. 49:5].

I submit this to you as being one of the most remarkable passages in the Word of God.

Thus saith the LORD, the Redeemer of Israel, and his Holy One, to him whom man despiseth, to him whom the nation abhorreth, to a servant of rulers, Kings shall see and arise, princes also shall worship, because of the LORD that is faithful, and the Holy One of Israel, and he shall choose thee [Isa. 49:7].

Paul said it like this: "Now if the fall of them be the riches of the world, and the diminishing of them the riches of the Gentiles; how much more their fulness?" (Rom. 11:12). The rejection of Christ by Israel meant that the gospel went to the ends of the earth. Just think how great it will be some day in the future when God regathers Israel!

DISCUSSION OF JEHOVAH WITH ISRAEL

From this section, the discussion of Jehovah with Israel regarding their restoration, I shall lift out only a few verses:

> **Thus saith the LORD, In an acceptable time have I heard thee, and in a day of salvation have I helped thee: and I will preserve thee, and give thee for a covenant of the people, to establish the earth, to cause to inherit the desolate heritages [Isa. 49:8].**

God heard the prayer of Christ, and He whom the nation crucified will be the One before whom kings will bow, and every knee must bow and acknowledge His Lordship.

> **Sing, O heavens; and be joyful, O earth; and break forth into singing, O mountains; for the LORD hath comforted his people, and will have mercy upon his afflicted [Isa. 49:13].**

God's purposes in the *earth* center in the nation Israel. When they are back in the land, then both the heavens and the earth can rejoice. Today, however, everything is more or less out of place as far as the world is concerned. Israel should be in their land, in the place of blessing, serving God. They are not. The church should be in heaven with Christ, but the church is still in the world. The Devil should be in hell, but he is walking around the earth seeking whom he may devour. The Lord Jesus Christ should be sitting upon the throne of the earth, ruling the earth, but He is at the right hand of God. There are many things that have to be shifted around and put in the right socket. Then the lines of Robert Browning as written in "Pippa Passes" will be true: "God's in His heaven: All's right with the world." At the moment, these words just do not fit the world in which you and I live.

Even the people of Israel think they are forsaken of God—

But Zion said, The Lord hath forsaken me, and my Lord hath forgotten me.

Can a woman forget her sucking child, that she should not have compassion on the son of her womb? yea, they may forget, yet will I not forget thee.

Behold, I have graven thee upon the palms of my hands; thy walls are continually before me [Isa. 49:14–16].

What beautiful assurance God gives them that they are not forsaken of Him! Israel may forsake Him—as they are doing yet today—but God will never forsake them.

My friend, if you still have doubts that God will restore Israel, I submit this section to you for your careful study.

DIGRESSION—JUDGMENT OF ISRAEL'S OPPRESSORS

Thus saith the Lord God, Behold I will lift up mine hand to the Gentiles, and set up my standard to the people: and they shall bring thy sons in their arms, and thy daughters shall be carried upon their shoulders [Isa. 49:22].

God assures Israel that the Gentiles will assist Him in the final restoration of the nation to the land. Heretofore, the Gentiles have *scattered* them, which makes this a rather remarkable prophecy even for today. Great Britain did open the land for the Jews; yet Great Britain was the country that issued the mandate which forbade them to enter the land—so they came by ship *without* permission, and they have been hindered in one way or another since that time. It has taken persecution to push them out of other countries, and at the time I am writing this they are being blocked from leaving Russia, which probably has the third largest Jewish population in the world. Russia doesn't want to get rid of them, yet it subjects them to a great deal of anti-Semitic oppression. However, in *that* day, that is, in the end times, God will bring them back into their land, and He will use Gentiles to move them back!

CHAPTER 50

THEME: The reason for the rejection of Israel: Israel's rejection of Christ

Israel's rejection of Christ is the real hurdle that they must get over before there can be blessing for them. He came as their Messiah; He actually was one of them. "He came unto his own, and his own received him not" (John 1:11). He came to His own people, and His own people did not receive Him.

GOD THE FATHER STATES THE REASON

Thus saith the LORD, Where is the bill of your mother's divorcement, whom I have put away? or which of my creditors is it to whom I have sold you? Behold, for your iniquities have ye sold yourselves, and for your transgressions is your mother put away [Isa. 50:1].

Under the Mosaic Law (see Deut. 24:1) a man could put away his wife on the slightest pretext. A cruel and hardhearted man would take advantage of this to get rid of his wife. God asks Israel if they know on what grounds He set them aside. Certainly God is not cruel or brutal. Israel is spoken of as the wife of Jehovah—this is the theme of Hosea. It was not a whim of God that caused Israel to be set aside, but God makes it very clear that their sin brought about their rejection.

Wherefore, when I came, was there no man? when I called, was there none to answer? Is my hand shortened at all, that it cannot redeem? or have I no power to deliver? behold, at my rebuke I dry up the sea, I make the rivers a wilderness: their fish stinketh, because there is no water, and dieth for thirst [Isa. 50:2].

"When I came"—when did Jehovah come directly to His people, not through His prophets but *Himself,* to Israel and expect such a welcome? It was not when He descended on Mount Sinai to give them the Mosaic Law. He looked for no welcome then, but insisted that they keep their distance. But He came again as a man, a humble man, and there was no reception of Him at all. Israel did not welcome Him at His birth; they didn't receive Him when He began His ministry. They rejected and killed their Messiah. Simon Peter on the Day of Pentecost put it like this: "Ye men of Israel, hear these words; Jesus of Nazareth, a man approved of God among you by miracles and wonders and signs, which God did by him in the midst of you, as ye yourselves also know: Him, being delivered by the determinate counsel and fore-knowledge of God, ye have taken, and by wicked hands have crucified and slain: Whom God hath raised up, having loosed the pains of death: because it was not possible that he should be holden of it" (Acts 2:22–24). God makes it very clear that because they rejected their Messiah, they have been set aside.

GOD THE SON SPEAKS OF HIS HUMILIATION

The Lord God hath given me the tongue of the learned, that I should know how to speak a word in season to him that is weary: he wakeneth morning by morning, he wakeneth mine ear to hear as the learned [Isa. 50:4].

The title by which Christ, the perfect Servant, addresses God is revealing. It is "Jehovah Adonai." The Lord Jesus Christ made Himself known to His people as "Jehovah Adonai." He came meek and lowly to do the Father's will.

"He wakeneth mine ear to *hear* as the learned" means the Lord Jesus was studying the Word of God. The question is asked, What did the Lord Jesus do the first thirty years of His life? Generally the answer is that he worked as a carpenter. But that is only half the truth. The other half is that He studied the Word of God. How tremendous! If *He* needed to study the Word of God, what about you? What about me? I think we need to get with it!

It is nonsense to say, "Oh, I believe the Bible from cover to cover; I will defend it with my life," when you don't study it! If God has spoken between the pages of Genesis 1:1 and Revelation 22:21, then somewhere between God has a word for you and for me. If God is speaking to us, we ought to listen.

The Lord GOD hath opened mine ear, and I was not rebellious, neither turned away back [Isa. 50:5].

This speaks of the Lord's true submission in His crucifixion. In Exodus 21:1-6 we are told that when a servant wanted to become a permanent servant, his master would bore or pierce a hole in his ear. "Then his master shall bring him unto the judges; he shall also bring him to the door, or unto the door post; and his master shall bore his ear through with an awl; and he shall serve him for ever" (Exod. 21:6). He could wear an earring after that, and I am convinced that he did. It indicated that he was a slave for life to his master.

Now the reason he would become a slave forever is twofold. First, he loved his master; and second, he had married a slave girl and he refused to go without her.

Do you see how this was applied to the Lord Jesus? The psalmist, referring to this custom, wrote, ". . . mine ears hast thou opened . . ." (Ps. 40:6). Now notice how this is quoted in Hebrews 10:5: "Wherefore when he cometh into the world, he saith, Sacrifice and offering thou wouldest not, but a body hast thou prepared me." In the psalm it says, "mine ears hast thou opened," and in Hebrews it says, "a body hast thou prepared me." When the Lord Jesus came down to this earth and went to the cross, His ear wasn't "opened" or "digged"; He was given a body, and that body was *nailed* to a cross. He has taken a glorified body bearing nail prints back to heaven. He did more than have his ear bored through with an awl; He gave His *body* to be *crucified* because He loved us and would not return to heaven without us!

I gave my back to the smiters, and my cheeks to them that plucked off the hair; I hid not my face from shame and spitting [Isa. 50:6].

This was literally fulfilled when Jesus was arrested. Matthew, Mark, and John all record the fact that He was spit upon, scourged, buffeted, and smitten. This is something we don't like to think about and would like to pass over, but it was literally fulfilled.

GOD THE HOLY SPIRIT SUGGESTS
MEN TRUST THE SON

Who is among you that feareth the LORD, that obeyeth the voice of his servant, that walketh in darkness, and hath no light? let him trust the name of the LORD, and stay upon his God [Isa. 50:10].

This is the wooing word. The Holy Spirit speaks a soothing and imploring word to trust and rest in God's Servant.

He turns from this and gives a warning word:

Behold, all ye that kindle a fire, that compass yourselves about with sparks: walk in the light of your fire, and in the sparks that ye have kindled. This shall ye have of mine hand; ye shall lie down in sorrow [Isa. 50:11].

First it is the wooing word as He implores them; then He gives a warning word to those who walk in the light of their own fire, rejecting the One who is the light of the world.

Some time ago a man said to me, "McGee, I heard you on the radio, and I disagree with you about salvation. Let me tell you what I think about it." Well, he was ready to build a fire, and he wanted both of us to sit there and warm ourselves by his fire. I knew it was a phony fire, which would give off no heat or light. So I frankly said to him, "I don't mean to be ugly or rude, but I don't want to hear what you think, because what you think and what I think are quite meaningless. It is what *God says* that we need to know." And we need to walk in the light of the Lord Jesus. He is the Light of the World. If we reject Him who is the Light of the World, then we generally walk in the light of our own little fire down here. The Holy Spirit gives this warning: You will lie down by that little fire of yours in sorrow, which means you will be eternally lost.

CHAPTER 51

THEME: *Israel's origin from past history; Israel's outlook for the future; outline of Israel's present conditions*

It is impossible to read this chapter without realizing that God has a future purpose for the nation Israel—just as He has a future purpose for the church and for you and me.

Let me remind you that the final verse of chapter 50 concluded with a warning, which might lead you to an amillennialist interpretation. God doesn't want us to hold the view that Israel as a nation has been set aside permanently and that when He speaks of Israel, He means the church. My friend, when God says *Israel,* He means *Israel.* If He had meant the church instead of Israel, somewhere along the line He would have said, "I hope you understand that when I say Israel I mean the church." No, He makes it very clear that He means Israel. Just as Israel has had a past rooted in a very small beginning, just so today they are small and set aside. But this does not mean God has forsaken them.

To illustrate this I use the figure of a train. God is running through the world a twofold program: One of them is expressed in the words, "Yet have I set my king upon my holy hill of Zion" (Ps. 2:6)—that train will be coming through later, but now it is on the side-track. On the main track He is ". . . bringing many sons unto glory" (Heb. 2:10), which refers to believers (or the church). When this train has come into the Union Station one time, God will put back on the main track the program of Israel and the gentile nations which are then upon the earth. And He is going to bring that train through on time also.

God's time piece is not B-U-L-O-V-A or G-R-U-E-N, but I-S-R-A-E-L. In this chapter God turns on the alarm to awaken those who are asleep that they might know that the eternal morning is coming soon. In Romans 13:11–12 we read, "And that, knowing the time, that now it is high time to awake out of sleep: for now is our salvation nearer than when we believed. The night is far spent, the day is at hand: let us therefore cast off the works of darkness, and let us put on the armour of light."

ISRAEL'S ORIGIN FROM PAST HISTORY

Hearken to me, ye that follow after righteousness, ye that seek the LORD: look unto the rock whence ye are hewn, and to the hole of the pit whence ye are digged [Isa. 51:1].

"Hearken to me," is God turning on the alarm. This is a call to every sincere heart in Israel that longs to be righteous and desires to know God. He says, "Wake up! Hear Me! I have a plan."

Look unto Abraham your father, and unto Sarah that bare you: for I called him alone, and blessed him, and increased him [Isa. 51:2].

God is saying, "I called Abraham when he was over in Chaldea in idolatry, and look what I've done through him! Now I want to move in your heart and life."

ISRAEL'S OUTLOOK FOR THE FUTURE

Hearken unto me, my people; and give ear unto me, O my nation: for a law shall proceed from me, and I will make my judgment to rest for a light of the people [Isa. 51:4].

"O my nation" is Israel. This is a word of glorious anticipation for them.

My righteousness is near; my salvation is gone forth, and mine arms shall judge the people; the isles shall

wait upon me, and on mine arm shall they trust [Isa. 51:5].

"My righteousness is near"—righteousness is Christ. He is made unto us "righteousness."

"The isles" are all the continents which are inhabited by the human family. God says, "I have a salvation which I will send out to them."

"On mine arm shall they trust"—the arm of God, as we shall see in Isaiah 53, is His salvation. The question is asked, "to whom is the [bared] arm of the LORD revealed?" (Isa. 53:1). God wants that bared arm of redemption in Christ to be revealed to the lost world. Therefore He is sending out this message that this bared arm will deliver Israel in the future.

Therefore the redeemed of the LORD shall return, and come with singing, unto Zion; and everlasting joy shall be upon their head: they shall obtain gladness and joy; and sorrow and mourning shall flee away [Isa. 51:11].

"Zion" is a geographical location (in Jerusalem) on *earth*. We need to understand that God means what He says here.

The captive exile hasteneth that he may be loosed, and that he should not die in the pit, nor that his bread should fail.

But I am the LORD thy God that divided the sea, whose waves roared: The LORD of hosts is his name [Isa. 51:14–15].

Just as God brought their father Abraham from the ends of the earth, God intends to bring Israel back to the land. This is what the prophet Jeremiah is saying: "But, The LORD liveth, which brought up and which led the seed of the house of Israel out of the north country, and from all countries whither I had driven them; and they shall dwell in their own land" (Jer. 23:8). The day will come when Israel will no longer remember the deliverance out of Egypt, so great will be their deliverance in the future. My friend, this is tremendous! You can't just set it aside and ignore it. God is saying, "Wake up! This is what I'm going to do."

OUTLINE OF ISRAEL'S PRESENT CONDITIONS

The present conditions of Israel ought to tell us something. God is still telling us to wake up.

> **Awake, awake, stand up, O Jerusalem, which hast drunk at the hand of the Lord the cup of his fury; thou hast drunken the dregs of the cup of trembling, and wrung them out [Isa. 51:17].**

All you have to do is look at Jerusalem today. It is a city in turmoil. I have no desire right now to stay there permanently, although it was a favorite spot of David, and it is also God's favorite spot on earth. But God has yet to make it beautiful. He has yet to bring His people there. God is saying, "Wake up, O Jerusalem. I am going to make you a great city."

> **Thus saith thy Lord the Lord, and thy God that pleadeth the cause of his people, Behold, I have taken out of thine hand the cup of trembling, even the dregs of the cup of my fury; thou shalt no more drink it again [Isa. 51:22].**

God has been pressing the cup of fury to their lips because of their rejection of Christ, but the day is coming when He will remove the cup. The day will come when God will take away judgment and bless them. How can you say that God is through with the nation Israel? Even poetic justice demands that after all these years of judgment upon the land and upon the people, God should bless them. God will get the victory, and that is what He is telling us here.

But I will put it into the hand of them that afflict thee; which have said to thy soul, Bow down, that we may go over; and thou hast laid thy body as the ground, and as the street, to them that went over [Isa. 51:23].

The enemies of Israel will not escape the judgment of God. Every nation that has majored in anti-Semitism has fallen: Egypt, Persia, Rome, Spain, Belgium, and Germany. This chapter should alert the believers today that God will yet choose Israel, and that the events in the Near East indicate that we are fast approaching the end times although no specific prophecy is being fulfilled in this hour.

CHAPTER 52

THEME: Invitation to the redeemed remnant of Israel; institution of the Kingdom to Israel; introduction of the suffering Servant

As we have been moving through Isaiah, we have seen in the shadows or in the background the Servant of Jehovah. Now as we approach chapter 53 we will see very clearly that the Servant of Jehovah is none other than our Lord Jesus Christ.

In the preceding chapter, the "alarm clock" chapter, the alarm was going off—"Awake, awake!" Now again in the chapter before us we have the alarm sounding.

INVITATION TO THE REDEEMED
REMNANT OF ISRAEL

Awake, awake; put on thy strength, O Zion; put on thy beautiful garments, O Jerusalem, the holy city: for henceforth there shall no more come into thee the uncircumcised and the unclean [Isa. 52:1].

When God says, "O Zion," He doesn't mean Los Angeles, or Pocatello, Idaho, or Muleshoe, Texas. He means *Zion*, which is a geographical place in the land of Israel. It is actually the hight point in the city of Jerusalem. It was David's favorite spot. Blessing is going to come upon Jerusalem, and it will no longer be an unattractive place. I was not impressed when I saw Jerusalem for the first time. I came up from Jericho and made that turn around the Mount of Olives by Bethany; then I was within sight of the temple area, the wall, and the east gate—that was a thrill. It was late in the afternoon and a shadow was over the city. I could hardly wait until the next morning to enter the city and visit around. Well, the next day was a great disappointment to me. That city is not beautiful in my opinion. Yet the Word of God says it is beautiful for situation; so that's God's viewpoint. I will agree with Him that the situation of it is beautiful, but not the city. However, He makes it clear here that it will be beautiful some day—because of our Lord's work of redemption. You see, Christ will redeem this physical universe, which now is groaning and travailing together in pain. All the world will become a beautiful spot because of redemption in Christ. He will redeem our bodies; we will get new bodies, and when this takes place, all creation will be redeemed. Redemption is not only of the person but of the property. This is the type of redemption that God permitted in the Mosaic Law, which serves as an illustration of it.

> **Shake thyself from the dust; arise, and sit down, O Jerusalem: loose thyself from the bands of thy neck, O captive daughter of Zion [Isa. 52:2].**

Today the Arab is there. All the sacred spots are covered with churches—Russian Orthodox, Greek Orthodox, Roman Catholic, Lutheran, and the Church of All Nations—they are all over the place! Jerusalem needs to be released from religion. It needs to be turned loose from the sin and the low degree of civilization that is there right now. Release is coming some day, and it will come during the Millennium. For twenty-five hundred years that city has been captive and trodden down of the Gentiles, but the day is coming when the shackles of slavery will be removed.

> **For thus saith the LORD, Ye have sold yourselves for nought; and ye shall be redeemed without money [Isa. 52:3].**

Since God received nothing from those who took His holy city captive, He will give nothing in return. He will take it from them and restore it again.

> **For thus saith the Lord GOD, My people went down aforetime into Egypt to sojourn there; and the Assyrian oppressed them without cause [Isa. 52:4].**

Jacob went down to Egypt by invitation, but his children were made slaves. The Assyrians, and others likewise, have oppressed them. That will end when the Millennium begins.

> **Now therefore, what have I here, saith the Lord, that my people is taken away for nought? they that rule over them make them to howl, saith the Lord; and my name continually every day is blasphemed [Isa. 52:5].**

God received no gain from the years of His people's rejection. Therefore He says:

> **Therefore my people shall know my name: therefore they shall know in that day that I am he that doth speak: behold, it is I [Isa. 52:6].**

This is a lovely thought! When the Lord was here over nineteen hundred years ago, they did not know Him. If they had only known the day of His visitation! Well, they *will* know Him when He comes again, and He will say, "Behold, it is I." This expression is rendered freely by Lowth: "Here I am." The world has rejected Christ; it doesn't know Him. One day He will say to the Christ-rejecting world, "Here I am," and it will be too late then for the multitudes who have rejected Him to turn to Him.

INSTITUTION OF THE KINGDOM TO ISRAEL

> **Break forth into joy, sing together, ye waste places of Jerusalem: for the Lord hath comforted his people, he hath redeemed Jerusalem [Isa. 52:9].**

One of the things you will note about the present-day Jerusalem is the lack of a joyful song. It is even true of the churches there. I listened for it but never heard a joyful song. Around the Mosque of Omar (which stands on the temple site) everything is in a minor key. If you go to the wailing wall, wailing is what you will hear, and the Jews are knocking their heads against it. But in the Millennium everybody is going to have fun—they will "Break forth into joy" and they will "sing together." It will be a joyous time!

Even today I don't think God likes to see us saints walking around with long faces, complaining and criticizing. He wants us to have joy. The apostle John wrote, "And these things write we unto you, that your joy may be *full*" (1 John 1:4, italics mine)—not just a little fun, but fun all the time!

The Millennium is the time when God answers the prayer which our Lord taught His disciples: "Thy kingdom come . . ." (Matt. 6:10). The tears and the sorrow will be gone; no longer will there be weeping on the earth. Instead there will be joy, and they will know that the millennial Kingdom has come.

INTRODUCTION OF THE SUFFERING SERVANT

My friend, somebody will have to travail if you are going to rejoice at a birth, a new birth and a new world. Therefore we have here the suffering of the Servant.

> **Behold, my servant shall deal prudently, he shall be exalted and extolled, and be very high [Isa. 52:13].**

Several of the administrations in Washington over the past few years have used the word *prudent* to excess. They speak of being prudent in their conduct. There is some question about whether they were prudent or not. If you think the Democrats have been prudent, ask the Republicans. If you think the Republicans have been prudent, ask the Democrats. You will find out that nobody has been prudent. Man today has not dealt prudently; but, when the Lord Jesus Christ comes, He will deal prudently. That is the picture we have here.

"He shall be exalted and extolled, and be very high." Paul writing to the Philippian believers says, "Wherefore God also hath highly exalted him, and given him a name which is above every name: that at the name of Jesus every knee should bow, of things in heaven, and things in earth, and things under the earth; and that every tongue should confess that Jesus Christ is Lord, to the glory of God the Father" (Phil. 2:9–11).

Now we see the suffering Servant—

As many were astonied at thee; his visage was so marred more than any man, and his form more than the sons of men [Isa. 52:14].

This is a picture of the crucifixion of Christ, and this statement prepares the way for chapter 53. I want to be careful, because it is not always a sign of orthodoxy to dwell upon the sufferings of Christ upon the Cross; sometimes it is only being crude.

During that time of darkness when men could no longer do anything, the Son of God was working on the Cross. It was during those three hours in blackness that the Cross became an altar and the Son of Man, the Lamb of God, paid for the sins of the world. After the three hours of darkness, the crowd must have been startled when the light broke upon the Cross. He did not even look human—just a bloody piece of quivering human flesh. It was unspeakable. We will see in the next chapter that there was "no beauty that we should desire him" (Isa. 53:2). That is the reason God put the mantle of darkness down on the Cross. There was nothing there to satisfy the morbid curiosity of man.

"His visage was so marred more than any man." When I was a pastor in Nashville, Tennessee, there was a wonderful elder on the church board who was a captain in the fire department. He always talked about the importance of having a first aid kit, and he taught classes in first aid. He asked me a dozen times if I had a first aid kit in my car, and because of his urging I finally got one. Early one morning there was a fire alarm and the firemen responded to the call. On the way to the fire, the hook and ladder truck on which he was riding was hit by a milk truck and flipped over. The men riding on it were dragged along the asphalt. I received a call about five o'clock in the morning and was told that he was in the hospital. He was still alive when I arrived, and his father was sitting beside his bed. When I looked at him I saw that his face was so marred that I didn't even recognize him.

All I could see was a mouth and I could tell that he was breathing—that was all. He didn't last very long. In an hour's time he was gone.

Many times since then I have thought of the fact that the Lord Jesus was marred more than any man, which means He had to be marred more than the captain of the fire company. He was just a piece of quivering human flesh. That is what my Lord went through on the Cross!

I don't feel that we should move into the realm of being crude in describing Him, because the next verse says:

So shall he sprinkle many nations; the kings shall shut their mouths at him: for that which had not been told them shall they see; and that which they had not heard shall they consider [Isa. 52:15].

"So shall he sprinkle many nations" could be translated, "So shall He make with astonishment many nations." This carries the thought that His death will *startle* people when they properly understand it. The death of Christ should never become commonplace to anyone. His death was different. We have not explained it properly unless it *startles* people.

This prepares us for the profound mystery of the next marvelous chapter.

CHAPTER 53

THEME: *The suffering of the Savior; the satisfaction of the Savior*

Those who are acquainted with God's Word realize that Isaiah 53 and Psalm 22 give us a more vivid account of the crucifixion of Christ than is found elsewhere in the Bible. This may be a shock to many who are accustomed to think that the four Gospels alone describe the sad episode of the horrible death of the Son of God. If you will examine the Gospel accounts carefully, you will make the discovery that only a few unrelated events connected with the Crucifixion are given and that the actual Crucifixion is passed over with reverent restraint. The Holy Spirit has drawn the veil of silence over that cross, and none of the lurid details are set forth for the curious mob to gaze at and leer upon. It is said of the brutal crowd who murdered Him that they sat down and watched Him. You and I are not permitted to join that crowd. Even they did not see all, for God placed over His Son's agony the mantle of darkness. Some sensational speakers gather to themselves a bit of notoriety by painting, with picturesque speech, the minutest details of what they *think* took place at the crucifixion of Christ. Art has given us the account of his death in ghastly reality. You and I probably will never know, even in eternity, the extent of His suffering.

> But none of the ransomed ever knew
> How deep were the waters crossed,
> Nor how dark was the night that the Lord passed thro'
> Ere He found His sheep that was lost.
> —Elizabeth C. Clephane,
> "The Ninety and Nine"

Very likely God did not want us to become familiar with that which we need not know. He did not wish us to treat as commonplace that which is so sacred. We should remind ourselves constantly of the danger of becoming familiar with holy things. "Be ye clean, that bear the vessels of the LORD" (Isa. 52:11).

Isaiah, seven hundred years before Christ was born, lets us see something of His suffering that we will not find anywhere else. Before going any further, we should pause a moment to answer the question that someone, even now, is doubtless asking: "How do you know that Isaiah is referring to the death of Christ? Isaiah wrote seven hundred years before Christ was born." Well, that is just the question that the Ethiopian eunuch raised when Philip hitchhiked a ride from him in the desert. The Ethiopian was going from Jerusalem back to his own country, and he was reading the fifty-third chapter of Isaiah. We are even told the very place in the chapter where he was reading (see Acts 8:32).

When I was a little boy in Sunday school, I was given a picture of the Ethiopian eunuch sitting in his chariot, holding in one hand the reins and in the other hand the book he was reading. Well, with a little thought we would realize that it couldn't have happened that way.

This man was an official of the government of Ethiopia. He was going across the desert in style. I am sure that he was under some sort of a shade as he sat there reading. He had a chauffeur who was doing the driving for him.

As the Ethiopian was reading Isaiah 53:7–8 his question to Philip was, ". . . I pray thee, of whom speaketh the prophet this? of himself, or of some other man?" (Acts 8:34). How can we be sure that Isaiah was referring to the Lord Jesus Christ in the fifty-third chapter? Listen to Philip. He will answer the Ethiopian's question and our question as well. "Then Philip opened his mouth, and began at the same scripture, and preached unto him Jesus" (Acts 8:35).

Also Christ Himself in John 12:38 quoted from Isaiah 53 and made application to Himself. And the apostle Paul in Romans 10:16 quotes from this same chapter in connection with the gospel of Christ. My friend, Scripture leaves no doubt that Isaiah 53 refers to Christ. Even more than that, it is a photograph of the Cross of Christ as He was dying there.

The first nine verses will tell us of the suffering of the Savior. The remainder of the chapter tells the satisfaction of the Savior.

You will find that these two themes belong together—suffering and satisfaction. Suffering always precedes satisfaction. Too many folk are trying to take a shortcut to happiness by attempting to avoid all the trying experiences of life. I want to tell you that there is no short route to satisfaction. This is the reason I condemn short-term courses that claim they have the answers to all of life's problems and will equip you with the whole armor of God. Well, that's not the way God does it. There is no short route. Even God did not go the short route. He could have avoided the Cross and accepted the crown. That was Satan's suggestion. But suffering always comes before satisfaction. Phraseology bears various expressions: through trial to triumph; sunshine comes after the clouds; light follows darkness; and flowers come after the rain. That seems to be God's way of doing things. Since it is His method, then it is the very best way. Perhaps you are sitting in the shadows of life today. Trials confront you, and problems overwhelm you, and the fiery furnace is your present lot, and you have tasted the bitter without the sweet. If that is your case right now, then let me encourage your heart and fortify your faith by saying that you are on the same pathway that God followed, and that it leads at last to light if you walk with Him. ". . . weeping may endure for a night, but joy cometh in the morning" (Ps. 30:5).

Now with this in mind, let's look at the suffering Savior.

THE SUFFERING OF THE SAVIOR

This chapter opens with the enigmatic inquiry:

> **Who hath believed our report? and to whom is the arm of the LORD revealed? [Isa. 53:1].**

The prophet seems to be registering a complaint because his message is not believed. That which was revealed to him is not received by men, and this is always the sad office of the prophet. When God called this man Isaiah, back in chapter 6, He told him, "You are going to get a message that the people won't hear. When you tell them My words, they won't believe you." That certainly was Isaiah's experience.

God's messengers have not been welcomed with open arms by the world. The prophets have been stoned and the message unheeded. That is still true today. After World War I, when everyone was talking about peace and safety, it was very, very unpopular even to suggest that there might be another war. Public opinion then demanded that we sink all the battleships and disarm ourselves, because our leaders told us that the world was safe for democracy. There were a few prophets of God in that period, standing in the pulpits of the land. They were not pacifists, but they did not care for war either. They declared in unmistakable terms that God's Word said there would be wars and rumors of war so long as there was sin, unrighteousness, and evil in the world. They stated that war was not a skin disease, but a heart disease, and they were proven correct when we entered World War II. When others declared that Christ was a pacifist, they called attention to the fact that He had said that a strong man armed keepeth his palace. I can recall that the church I attended as a boy had just such a minister. He was a faithful servant of Christ, and he sought to please God rather than men. But his message was largely rejected, and he was not popular with the crowd—they preferred the liberal preacher in the town. But time has now proven that he was right, and current events demonstrate that he was a friend of this nation, not an enemy. He was a prophet of God and could say with Isaiah, "Who has believed our report?" There are a few prophetic voices lifted up right now in America. They are trying to call this nation back to God before it is too late, but the crowd is rushing headlong after another delusion.

Personally I am overwhelmed by the marvelous response to our Bible teaching program on radio. But every now and then we are reminded that we are in a Christ-rejecting world. Our program has been put off the air by several radio stations because they did not like our message. One radio manager called in to say that he did not like the kind of "religion" I was preaching. He wanted to know if it would be possible to give something a little bit more cheerful, because mankind was on the up-and-up and getting better and better. They weren't sinners, and things were not as bad as I seemed to think they were. This man's call, and others like it, simply serve to remind us that we are in a Christ-rejecting world, and we must accept it as such and keep on going. We rejoice today that we have as large an outlet as we do. I believe that there are many prophetic voices in our nation today trying to call us back to God before it is too late. In spite of that, the majority of the people are following any Pied Piper of liberalism who has a tune they can jig by and who makes them feel like everything is going to be all right.

Paul said the preaching of the Cross is to them that perish foolishness. From ideas publicly expressed we are given to know that there are many to whom the preaching of the Cross is foolishness. I admit there is a lot of foolish preaching and offer no apology for it. But God said they would identify the preaching of the Cross with foolishness. This message is a challenge to those folk, for there is a reason for them thinking as they do. God says, "But the natural man receiveth not the things of the Spirit of God: for they are foolishness unto him: neither can he know them, because they are spiritually discerned" (1 Cor. 2:14). Would that they would give God a chance to talk with them!

It must be remembered that God does not use man's methods and ways to accomplish things. God chooses the weak things of the world to confound the mighty and the foolish things to confound the wise. If we were to call in a specialist in a time of illness, we certainly would not expect him to use the same home remedies normally used by us. His procedure might appear foolish to us, but we would follow it faithfully. Then should we not accord to God the same dealing of fairness as we do to the specialist?

But we still have to say with Isaiah, "Who hath believed our report? and to whom is the arm of the LORD revealed?"

There is a very definite reason why men do not believe in God's gospel. Men like to think of God as sitting somewhere in heaven upon some lofty throne. The ancients spoke of the gods whose dwelling was not with mankind. The Greeks placed their deities upon Mount Olympus, and the Romans had Jupiter hurling thunderbolts from the battlements of the clouds. It is foreign to the field of religion that God has come down to this earth among men and that He suffered upon the shameful Cross. That is too much to comprehend. The modern mind calls that defeatism—they do not care for it. A suffering deity is contrary to man's thinking.

However, there is a peculiar fascination about this fifty-third chapter of Isaiah. There we see one suffering as no one else ever suffered. There we behold One in pain as a woman in travail. We are strangely drawn to Him and His cross. He said, "And I, if I be lifted up from the earth, will draw all men unto me" (John 12:32). Suffering has a singular attraction. Pain draws us all together. When you and I see some poor creature groaning in misery and covered with blood, our hearts instinctively go out in sympathy to the unfortunate victim. Somehow we want to help. That is the reason the Red Cross makes such an appeal to our hearts. Our sympathy is keen toward those who are war's victims, or the victims of twentieth century civilized barbarism. Pain places all of us on the same plane. It is a common bond uniting all the frail children of suffering humanity. Therefore look with me upon the strange sufferings of the Son of God. Let Him draw our cold hearts into the warmth of His sacrifice and the radiance of His love.

Isaiah enlarges upon his first question by asking further, "To whom is the [bared] arm of the LORD revealed?" "Bared arm" means that God has rolled up His sleeve, symbolic of a tremendous undertaking. When God created the heavens and the earth, it is suggested that it was merely His *fingerwork*. For instance, Psalm 19:1—"The heavens declare the glory of God; and the firmament sheweth his handiwork." That word *handiwork* is literally "fingerwork." Dr. T. DeWitt Talmage used to say that God created the physical universe without half trying. When God created the heavens and the earth, it was without effort. He merely *spoke* them into existence. When He rested on the seventh day, He wasn't tired; he had just finished everything; it was completed. But when God redeemed man, it required His "bared arm," for salvation was His greatest undertaking. One of the objections offered to God's salvation is that it is *free*. If by that is meant that for man it is free, then this is correct. Man can pay nothing, nor does he have anything to offer for salvation. The reason that it is free for man is because it cost God everything. He had to bare His arm. He gave His Son to die upon the cross. Redemption is an infinite task that only God could perform. Salvation is free, but it certainly is not cheap.

Now we have brought before us the person of Christ. We are told something of His origin on the human side.

For he shall grow up before him as a tender plant, and as a root out of a dry ground: he hath no form nor comeliness; and when we shall see him, there is no beauty that we should desire him [Isa. 53:2].

Christ was a root out of a dry ground. This means that at the time of the birth of Christ the family of David had been cut off from the kingship. They were no longer princes; they were peasants. The nation Israel was under the iron heel of Rome. They were not free. The Roman Empire produced no great civilization. They merely were good imitators of great civilizations. There was mediocre achievement and pseudoculture. The moral foundation was gone. A virile manhood and a virtuous womanhood was supplanted by a debauched and pleasure-loving citizenry. The religion of Israel had gone to seed. They merely performed an empty ritual, and their hearts remained cold and indifferent. Into such a situation Christ came. He came from a noble family that was cut off, from a nation that had become a vassal to Rome, in a day and age that was decadent. The loveliest flower of humanity came from the driest spot and period of the world's history. It was humanly impossible for His day and generation to produce Him, but He came nevertheless, for He came forth from God.

Let me use a ridiculous illustration. Christ coming where He did and when He did would be like our walking out in the desert in Arizona, without a green sprig anywhere, and suddenly coming upon a great big head of iceberg lettuce growing right out of that dry, dusty soil. We would be amazed. We would say, "How in the world can this head of lettuce grow out here?" It would be a miracle. The coming of Christ was just like that. His day could never have produced Him. Evolution has always tried to get rid of the Lord Jesus, because it cannot produce a Jesus. If it can, why doesn't it? The interesting thing is that He is different. Therefore He is the root out of a dry ground.

Now the prophet focuses our attention immediately upon His suffering and death upon the cross.

"He hath no form nor comeliness [majesty]; and when we shall see him, there is no beauty that we should desire him." Some have drawn the inference from this statement that Christ was unattractive and misshapen in some way. Some even dare to suggest that He was repulsive in His personal appearance. That cannot be true because He was the perfect man. The Gospel records do not lend support to any such viewpoint. It was on the cross that this declaration of Him became true in a very real way. His suffering was so intense that He became drawn and misshapen. The cross was not a pretty thing; it was absolutely repulsive to view. Men have fashioned crosses that look very attractive, but they do not represent His cross. His cross was not good to look upon; His suffering was unspeakable; His death was horrible. He endured what no other man endured. He did not even look human after the ordeal of the cross as we saw in the previous chapter. He was a mass of unsightly flesh.

Naturally, we are eager to learn why His death was different and horrible. What is the meaning of the depths of His suffering?

Surely he hath borne our griefs, and carried our sorrows: yet we did esteem him stricken, smitten of God, and afflicted [Isa. 53:4].

He was "smitten of God, and afflicted." The prophet was so afraid that you and I would miss this that he mentioned it three times: "The LORD hath laid on him the iniquity of us all." "Yet it pleased the LORD to bruise Him." "He hath put him to grief." Consternation fills our souls when we recognize that it was God the Father who treated the perfect Man in such terrible fashion.

Candidly, we do not understand it, and we are led to inquire why God should treat Him in this manner. What had he done to merit such treatment? Look for a moment at that cross. Christ was on the cross six hours, hanging between heaven and earth from nine o'clock in the morning until three o'clock in the afternoon. In the first three hours man did his worst. He heaped ridicule and insult upon Him, spit upon Him, nailed Him without mercy to the cruel cross, and then sat down to watch Him die. At twelve o'clock noon, after He had hung there for three hours in agony, God drew a veil over the sun, and darkness covered that scene, shutting out from human eye the transaction between the Father and the Son. Christ became the sacrifice for the sin of the world. God made His soul an offering for sin. Christ Jesus was treated as sin, for we are told that He was made sin for us who knew no sin. If you want to know if God hates sin, look at the Cross. If you want to know if God will punish sin, look at the Darling of His heart enduring the tortures of its penalty. By what vain conceit can you and I hope to escape if we neglect so great a salvation? That cross became an altar where we behold the Lamb of God taking away the sin of the world. He was dying for somebody else—He was dying for you and me.

Listen to the prophet:

But he was wounded for our transgressions, he was bruised for our iniquities: the chastisement of our peace was upon him; and with his stripes we are healed.

All we like sheep have gone astray; we have turned every one to his own way; and the LORD hath laid on him the iniquity of us all [Isa. 53:5–6].

The phrase "with His stripes we are healed" may cause questions in your mind. Of what are we healed? Are we healed of physical diseases? Is that the primary meaning of it? I am going to let Simon Peter interpret this by the inspiration of the Spirit of God. First Peter 2:24 says, "Who his own self bare our sins in his own body on the tree, that we, being dead to sins, should live unto righteousness: by whose stripes ye were healed." Healed of what? Peter makes it quite clear that we are healed of our trespasses and sins. Now notice that marvelous sixth verse. It begins with "all" and ends with "all." "All we like sheep have gone astray"—not some of us, but all of us. What is really the problem with mankind? What is your basic and my basic problem? It is stated in this clause: "We have turned every one to his own way." That is our problem. Man has gone *his* way, neglecting *God's* way. And the Scripture further says: "There is a way which seemeth right unto a man, but the end thereof are the ways of death" (Prov. 14:12). Another proverb admonishes: "In all thy ways acknowledge him, and he shall direct thy paths" (Prov. 3:6). Although our Lord Jesus said, ". . . I am the way, the truth and the life: no man cometh unto the Father, but by me" (John 14:6), we have turned every one to his own way.

"And the LORD hath laid on him the iniquity of us all." Isaiah is making it clear that when Christ died on the cross He was merely taking your place and mine. He had done nothing amiss. He was holy, harmless, undefiled, separate from sinners. He was the Substitute whom the love of God provided for the salvation of you and me.

Surely our hearts go out in sympathy to Him as He expired there upon the tree. Certainly we are not unmoved at such pain and suffering. We would be cold-blooded, indeed, if our own hearts were not responsive. It is said that when Clovis, the leader of the Franks, was told about the crucifixion of Christ, he was so moved that he leaped to his feet, drew his sword, and exclaimed, "If I had only been there with my Franks!" Yet, my friend, Christ does not want your sympathy. He did not die to win that. He didn't die to enlist us in His defense. Remember that when He was on the way to the cross and the women of Jerusalem were weeping for Him, He said, ". . . weep not for me, but weep for yourselves, and for your children. . . . For if they do these things in a green tree, what shall be done in the dry?" (Luke 23:28, 31). He did not want their sympathy, and He does not want ours.

Someone may be thinking that He died a martyr's death. He did not die a martyr's death, for He did not espouse a lost cause! He did not die as martyrs who in their death sang praises of joy and confessed that Christ was standing by them. Compare His death to that of Stephen's. Stephen in triumph said, ". . . Behold, I see the heavens opened, and the Son of man standing on the right hand of God" (Acts 7:56). Our Lord didn't die like that. He was *forsaken* of God. He said, ". . . My God, my God, why hast thou forsaken me?" (Matt. 26:46).

His death was different. He died alone—alone with the sins of the world upon Him.

Someone else may feel like saying what a wonderful influence the death of Christ should exercise upon our lives. As we contemplate His life and death, most assuredly we ought to be persuaded to turn from sin. However, that has not been the experience of men. By the way, how did it work in your life? That view will not satisfy as an explanation of this verse: "All we like sheep have gone astray; we have turned everyone to his own way; and the LORD hath laid on him the iniquity of us all." None of these will suffice to explain His death, for He is the Lamb of God that taketh away the sin of the world. He took our place.

THE SATISFACTION OF THE SAVIOR

At this point let me quote verse 3, which speaks of Christ's grief.

He is despised and rejected of men; a man of sorrows, and acquainted with grief: and we hid as it were our faces from him; he was despised, and we esteemed him not [Isa. 53:3].

Christ is identified as "a man of sorrows, and acquainted with grief," and the inference is that Christ was a very unhappy Man while He was here upon this earth. To fortify this position a few isolated incidents are quoted which speak of His weeping. Now I want to correct this impression if I can. In verse 4 it says that "he hath borne our griefs, and carried our sorrows." Notice that it was *our* sorrows and *our* griefs that He bore. He had no grief or sorrow of His own. He was supremely happy in His mission here upon earth. In the Epistle to the Hebrews it is said of Him ". . . for the *joy* that was set before him he endured the cross" (Heb. 12:2, italics mine). These pictures that show Him looking long-faced and very solemn misrepresent Him. Even on the cross He joyfully took our place. He made that cross an altar upon which He offered a satisfactory payment for the penalty of your sins and mine. *Willingly* He died there, for in verse 7 we read, "as a sheep before her shearers is dumb, so he openeth not his mouth."

Perhaps you are saying to yourself, "Preacher, that does not make sense to me. I do not believe that, nor do I care for that sort of religion. I do not want God to make a sacrifice for me. I did not ask Him to do it." Well, it is true that you did not ask Him to do it, but let me ask you a very plain and fair question. I am sure that you will agree that man has gotten this world into a very sad predicament today. The wisdom of man has failed to settle the issues of this life. Have you ever thought that man may be wrong about the next life when he dismisses God's remedy with a snap of the fingers? Vain philosophy and false science have not solved the problems of daily living. Since they are wrong in so many other areas, they may also be wrong about the Bible.

Suppose for a moment that God *did* give His Son to die for you and that He *did* make a tremendous sacrifice. Grant that the Cross is God's remedy for the sin of the world and that it is the very best that even God can do. Suppose also that you go on rejecting this gracious offer of salvation. Do you think that you can reasonably expect God to do anything for you in eternity? If God exhausted His love, His wisdom, and His power in giving Christ to die and patiently has waited for you to turn to Him, what else can He do to save you? What else do you suppose God can do for you, or for anyone, who rejects His Son? He would come again at this moment and die again if that would be the means to save you! It is no light thing to turn down God's love gift to you.

This does not end the gospel story. We do not worship a dead Christ; we worship a *living* One. He not only died, He rose again from the grave in victory. He ascended back into heaven. At this moment He is sitting at God's right hand, and the prophet says:

He shall see of the travail of his soul, and shall be satis-fied: by his knowledge shall my righteous servant jus-tify many; for he shall bear their iniquities [Isa. 53:11].

We have a living and rejoicing Savior, for His suffering led to *satisfac-tion*. He took our hell that we might have His heaven. He is happy, for down through the ages multitudes, yes, millions, have come to Him and found sweet release from guilt, pardon for wrongdoing, and healing from the leprosy of sin. Christ said there is *joy* in heaven over one sinner that repenteth, and that number can be multiplied by millions. Think of the joy and satisfaction of Christ today! We have a happy Christ, a joyful Christ, and it is going to be fun to be in His presence.

You can bring added joy to His heart by accepting the gift of eternal life that He longs to give to you. He is not asking anything of you—He wants to give you something. It is for ". . . him that worketh not, but believeth on him that justifieth the ungodly, his faith is counted for righteousness" (Rom. 4:5). All you have to do is accept Him right where you are. He invites you to the foot of the cross where you will find forgiveness for your sins. May this be your prayer and mine:

> Beneath the cross of Jesus
> I fain would take my stand—
> The shadow of a mighty Rock
> Within a weary land;
> A home within the wilderness,
> A rest upon the way,
> From the burning of the noontide heat,
> And the burden of the day.
>
> Upon the cross of Jesus
> Mine eye at times can see
> The very dying form of One
> Who suffered there for me:
> And from my stricken heart with tears
> Two wonders I confess—
> The wonders of redeeming love
> And my unworthiness.
> —Elizabeth C. Clephane,
> "Beneath the Cross of Jesus"

What a marvelous prayer this is for a sinner to pray! It makes it very clear that all men will not be saved, that all men must accept the Substitute or they will be lost. It also makes clear that the total depravity of man is taught in the Bible, that we are in no condition to save ourselves. All without exception are involved in guilt, and all without exception are involved in sin, and all without exception are guilty of straying, and all without exception have turned away from God, and all without exception have chosen their own way.

CHAPTER 54

THEME: The regathered and restored wife of Jehovah; the rejoicing and righteous restored wife of Jehovah

This is the logical chapter to follow Isaiah 53, because it is the song that accompanies salvation and the future glories of Israel. You see, the Redeemer is coming to Zion, and some day they will behold Him.

THE REGATHERED AND RESTORED WIFE OF JEHOVAH

He is speaking directly to Israel saying they should sing.

Sing, O barren, thou that didst not bear; break forth into singing, and cry aloud, thou that didst not travail with child: for more are the children of the desolate than the children of the married wife, saith the LORD [Isa. 54:1].

I can't sing. If you can, that's wonderful. But some day I am going to be able to sing. Redemption brings a song into the world. The world produces the blues; the redeemed sing of blessings. The world has its rock; the redeemed sing of redemption. The world plays jazz; the redeemed have the reality of joy. Only the redeemed have a song of joy. The redeemed will sing the song of redemption whether on earth or in heaven. "And they sung a new song, saying, Thou art worthy to take the book, and to open the seals thereof: for thou wast slain, and hast redeemed us to God by thy blood out of every kindred, and tongue, and people, and nation; And hast made us unto our God kings and priests: and we shall reign on the earth" (Rev. 5:9–10). What a picture we have here! You see, it is the church mentioned in Revelation, but in Isaiah 54 it is the nation Israel. The church is called a chaste virgin while Israel is characterized as the restored wife.

"Sing, O barren." In the past Israel has been as a barren wife. Sarah's life was this in miniature. She was barren, childless, an old woman ninety years old with no children. God caused the barren to bring forth a son, and just think of the millions that have come from her!

So the first word after the crucifixion in chapter 53 is "Sing." It is a call to Israel to sing. But the Jews are not singing over in their land today. In the past Israel has been as a barren wife, but in the future her travailing will be over. Her travailing so far has produced only wind—like the mountain that travailed and brought forth a mouse! But her future is glorious because she will have many children in the future.

> **Enlarge the place of thy tent, and let them stretch forth the curtains of thine habitations: spare not, lengthen thy cords, and strengthen thy stakes [Isa. 54:2].**

The nation Israel has never occupied the entire land given to them by the Lord. The land God marked out for them in Joshua 1:4 is about 300,000 square miles. Even in Israel's heyday, when they reached their zenith under David and Solomon, they only occupied 30,000 square miles—that is quite a difference. Now God says they are going to lengthen their cords and strengthen their stakes. And they are going to be safe in the land. They won't need to be afraid of the Arab in that day. During the Millennium, Israel will occupy the total borders of the land. Also, the city of Jerusalem will push out into the suburban areas, and there will be no traffic jams.

> **For thou shalt break forth on the right hand and on the left; and thy seed shall inherit the Gentiles, and make the desolate cities to be inhabited [Isa. 54:3].**

The Gentiles have occupied most of the Land of Promise—they have it today. But they will have to withdraw to their own borders. The problem in the world today is not only that individuals are trying to step over into somebody else's territory, but nations are trying to expand their borders. This causes problems. People just keep wanting more and more and more, which is what produces wars.

> **For thy Maker is thine husband; the LORD of hosts is his name; and thy Redeemer the Holy One of Israel; The God of the whole earth shall he be called [Isa. 54:5].**

God will own them then as His redeemed in that day.

> **For the LORD hath called thee as a woman forsaken and grieved in spirit, and a wife of youth, when thou wast refused, saith thy God [Isa. 54:6].**

Israel is today like a wife that has been divorced for adultery. That is the figure of speech that is used.

> **For a small moment have I forsaken thee; but with great mercies will I gather thee [Isa. 54:7].**

In that day not only Israel, but all of us are going to look back at what we thought was terrible down here in this life, and it will seem as Paul described it "a light affliction, which is but for a moment." And it will work for us an "exceeding and eternal weight of glory." We need to get our eyes focused on things which are not seen rather than things that are seen (see 2 Cor. 4:17–18).

> **For the mountains shall depart, and the hills be re-moved; but my kindness shall not depart from thee, nei-ther shall the covenant of my peace be removed, saith the LORD that hath mercy on thee [Isa. 54:10].**

If you feel that God is going to break His covenant which He made with Abraham, Isaiah would have you know that you are wrong. God will not break His covenant; He will never break it.

THE REJOICING AND RIGHTEOUS
RESTORED WIFE OF JEHOVAH

O thou afflicted, tossed with tempest, and not comforted, behold, I will lay thy stones with fair colours, and lay thy foundations with sapphires [Isa. 54:11].

Now God begins to comfort Israel that she might rejoice.

And all thy children shall be taught of the LORD; and great shall be the peace of thy children [Isa. 54:13].

This is the day when the knowledge of the Lord shall cover the earth. This brings peace.

In righteousness shalt thou be established: thou shalt be far from oppression; for thou shalt not fear: and from terror; for it shall not come near thee [Isa. 54:14].

Following righteousness is freedom from fear.
Now notice this marvelous verse of Scripture.

No weapon that is formed against thee shall prosper; and every tongue that shall rise against thee in judgment thou shalt condemn. This is the heritage of the servants of the LORD, and their righteousness is of me, saith the LORD [Isa. 54:17].

Even in the past and in the present, God has been opposed to anti-Semitism. No enemy of God's chosen nation has ever prospered. The witnesses to this truth are Pharaoh, Haman, Herod, and Hitler. There are a lot of anti-Semites in this country who ought to read this verse. This verse is a promise of God.

CHAPTER 55

THEME: *Invitation to the world; the ways of God; institution of the Word of God*

The work of the suffering Servant in chapter 53 makes possible the offer of salvation in this chapter. In chapter 54 the invitation was confined to Israel. In this chapter the invitation is extended to the entire world. The gospel went first to Israel and then to the Gentiles. I think this is what Paul meant when he said, "For I am not ashamed of the gospel of Christ: for it is the power of God unto salvation to every one that believeth; to the Jew first, and also to the Greek" (Rom. 1:16). This does not mean that the Jew has top priority today, but he shouldn't have bottom priority either; he is on the same par as everyone else. The Jew did receive the gospel first. Peter on the day of Pentecost preached to an all-Jewish congregation—there wasn't a Gentile in the lot. Now this invitation goes out to the *world*. This is remarkable because there have been very few religious leaders who have had a global view. The work of the suffering Servant in chapter 53 makes possible now the offer of salvation to a lost world.

God's invitation has yet to find its complete fulfillment in Israel. Today it is worldwide, with only one condition, as we shall see. This is not a mechanical offer locked in the airtight compartment of God's election, but it rests upon the free-flowing will of each hearer. He is urged—in fact, he is commanded—to seek the Lord.

INVITATION TO THE WORLD

Ho, every one that thirsteth, come ye to the waters, and he that hath no money; come ye, buy, and eat; yea, come, buy wine and milk without money and without price [Isa. 55:1].

The chapter opens with the heart cry of God to *every one* to pause and consider His salvation.

"Ho" is like a startled cry for help in the night. He wants every weak soul to behold His mighty bared arm of salvation.

The invitation is ecumenical. I don't believe in the ecumenical movement that men talk about today, but I do believe in God's ecumenical movement, which is that the invitation of the gospel is to go out to the world. However, it is limited to one class: "Ho, every one that thirsteth." This invitation is to every man, woman, and child on the topside of the earth. It means every man of every station in life, in all strata of society, from every race, tribe, tongue, condition, and color. All are included. The invitation is "Ho, every one."

But notice that it is limited to only certain ones—"every one that *thirsteth.*" It is for those whose thirst has not been slaked by the manmade cisterns and bars of this earth. The invitation is to drink deep and long of the eternal springs. Dr. F. C. Jennings has written: "Let us listen then, as if we had never heard the melody of this tender and gracious invitation before. Who are the guests here invited? *All who thirst!* All that is needed to be welcome then, is—not to *need* (for that is true of all)—but to *want* what is offered. Am I utterly dissatisfied with myself? I thirst! Am I dissatisfied with all the world can offer me, and of which I have tasted? I thirst! Is my spirit altogether dissatisfied with all the formalism of religion? Then do I thirst! Blessed thirst! It is the only prerequisite to enjoyment!" (*Studies in Isaiah,* p. 645).

This is the invitation: "Ho, everyone that thirsteth." If you say, "I am not interested. I am not thirsty. I am satisfied with the things of this life," then it is not for you, my friend. It is not for you until you are thirsty. Here in California you will be riding along in the desert and all of a sudden you will see on a billboard a picture of a bottle pushed down into some cracked ice. My, it looks good! There is only one word printed on the sign—"THIRSTY?" The company that put up the sign hopes you are thirsty. They want you to stop at the next service station and buy a coke or whatever they are selling. If you have your thermos bottles filled with iced tea, or orange juice, you say, "I am not thirsty," and drive on. But if you are thirsty, you will pull off at the next service station and get your drink.

At the crossroads of life God has put up a sign: "THIRSTY?" Ho, every one that is thirsty. Are you tired of this world? Have you found that it does not satisfy? Do you long for something better? God says, "I have something for you." Then He mentions a variety of things and says that you can buy these things without money. A bottled drink used to cost a nickel, now you are to pay forty cents and by the time you read this, the price may have gone even higher. But God's offer is without money. Why? Because back in Isaiah 53 the Lord Jesus paid the price for it on the Cross. This is God's invitation to you, "Come ye, buy, and eat." Not only drink, but He offers the bread of life, too.

Notice that there are three types of drink offered:

1. "Waters"—the plural form is used. In the Hebrew the plural expresses a superlative degree. This water is too wonderful to be expressed by the singular form. "Waters" also speaks of abundance, of quantity as well as quality. This is water for the *soul*. This is the kind of water that the Lord Jesus offered—and He used the same symbolism—when he stood in the temple area that day and cried, ". . . If any man thirst, let him come unto me, and drink" (John 7:37). Now we know where the fountain is—that fountain is Christ, who is the Water of Life and our Savior.

2. "Wine" is the second type of drink offered, which symbolizes joy. In Proverbs 31:6 we read, "Give strong drink unto him that is ready to perish, and wine unto those that be of heavy hearts." And 1 Thessalonians 1:6 says, "And ye became followers of us, and of the Lord, having received the word in much affliction, with *joy* of the Holy Ghost" (italics mine). Joy is what you have when Christ is not only your Savior but when He becomes the Master of your life. When you come to *know* Him, you have joy. In 1 John 1:4 John says, "And these things write we unto you, that your *joy* may be full" (italics mine). I saw this motto in a preacher's study in Salem, Oregon: "Joy is the flag that is flown in the heart when the Master is in residence." That is a marvelous drink that will put genuine joy in your heart!

3. "Milk" is the third type of drink offered. Milk is essential for growth and development, especially for babies. The dairy industry has been trying to tell people: "Every body needs milk." Well, the milk of the Word of God is essential for spiritual growth. Now, since I am a teacher of the Word of God, that makes me a milkman. I give out

the milk of the Word. Peter said it like this, "As newborn babes, desire the sincere milk of the word, that ye may grow thereby" (1 Pet. 2:2). Have you ever seen a little baby while his mama gets his bottle ready? That hungry little fellow, lying in his crib, is wiggling his feet, his hands; in fact, he is wiggling all over. With his mouth he is making all kinds of commotion and a great deal of noise! Why? Because he desires milk. And a child of God ought to want the milk of the Word of God with equal longing! My friend, if you are a believer, there is something wrong with you if you don't like to study the Word of God. The greatest problem in our churches today is that we are entertaining, we are giving nice little courses in this and that and the other thing, we are giving banquets and dinners, and we are putting folk on committees. We are doing everything but giving them the Word of God. Many church members are stillborn—they have no spiritual life. My friend, if you are a believer, you ought to want the sincere milk of the Word of God.

Wherefore do ye spend money for that which is not bread? and your labour for that which satisfieth not? hearken diligently unto me, and eat ye that which is good, and let your soul delight itself in fatness [Isa. 55:2].

Many folk, even Christians today, are spending money for so-called Christian enterprises that don't feed anybody. I hear some people today calling money bread—I rather like that expression. The Word of God is "bread" also. A lot of Christians put their money into that which is not bread, although they think it is. It would be well to investigate where you give your money. It may be that you are buying a load of sawdust, which won't satisfy your heart and life.

The question is asked, "Wherefore do ye spend money for that which is not bread?" The pleasures of this world are expensive. You have to pay for them. Not only are they expensive, but they never satisfy. They are counterfeit. They are sawdust and cannot satisfy the soul. Then where is happiness? You won't find it in money. Jay Gould, an American millionaire, had plenty of that. When he was dying, he said: "I suppose that I am the most miserable devil on earth." You won't find happiness in pleasure either. Lord Byron had fame, genius, money, and lived a life of pleasure, yet he wrote in his poem "On My Thirty-sixth Year": "The worm, the canker, and the grief are mine alone."

Why don't you come to the table where you can get some water, wine, milk, and bread that satisfies? That's where we all need to be today.

> Incline your ear, and come unto me: hear, and your soul shall live; and I will make an everlasting covenant with you, even the sure mercies of David [Isa. 55:3].

God was merciful to David, and He will be merciful to you and me today. I heard a man speaking in Pershing Square in Los Angeles one day, deriding and ridiculing the Bible. One Sunday evening I saw him in church when I was a pastor in downtown Los Angeles. After the service he came to talk to me, feigning a humble approach, and said, "Pastor, I have a question to ask you. Why did God choose a man like David?" Then he leered at me, and I knew exactly what the old rascal was thinking. I said, "I'll tell you why God chose a man like David. It was so that you and I would have the courage to come to Him. If God would take David, He might take *you*, and he might take *me!*" The sure mercies of David—how wonderful they are!

> Behold, I have given him for a witness to the people, a leader and commander to the people [Isa. 55:4].

Jesus is called the true witness for us in our day.

> Behold, thou shalt call a nation that thou knowest not, and nations that knew not thee shall run unto thee because of the Lord thy God, and for the Holy One of Israel; for he hath glorified thee [Isa. 55:5].

"Behold, thou shalt call a nation that thou knowest not"—at that time Isaiah didn't know about the United States of America, but we are included in his prophecy.

THE WAYS OF GOD

Seek ye the LORD while he may be found, call ye upon him while he is near [Isa. 55:6].

The way of God and the way of man are put in contrast and conflict. The objection is often made that this is not a legitimate gospel call for today since man is not asked to seek God, but rather God is seeking man. This certainly is accurate, but nonetheless this call is for today, as the human aspect is in view here. Human responsibility is not defeated by the sovereign purposes and election of God. Therefore the Lord Jesus could say, "All that the Father giveth me shall come to me; and him that cometh to me I will in no wise cast out" (John 6:37). You can sit on the sidelines and argue that you are not one of the elect; but the minute you come, you are a member of the elect. And the coming is up to you.

Let the wicked forsake his way, and the unrighteous man his thoughts: and let him return unto the LORD, and he will have mercy upon him; and to our God, for he will abundantly pardon [Isa. 55:7].

The problem people have today is not mental. You may say, "I have great intellectual hurdles to surmount before I can come to Christ." No, you don't. You have only one—that is sin in your life that you don't want to give up. That is the one thing that keeps men from God. "Let the wicked forsake his way," and when you do, then you will be ready to turn to Him. That is when you really get thirsty.

Now God says—

For my thoughts are not your thoughts, neither are your ways my ways, saith the LORD [Isa. 55:8].

God's way is different from man's way. The gospel is God's way. It is not man-made. No man could ever have devised it. "But I certify you, brethren, that the gospel which was preached of me is not after man. For I neither received it of man, neither was I taught it, but by the revelation of Jesus Christ" (Gal. 1:11–12). The gospel came down from heaven. It is God's gospel.

> **For as the heavens are higher than the earth, so are my ways higher than your ways, and my thoughts than your thoughts [Isa. 55:9].**

The gospel could come only by revelation, since man's reason never follows the redemption route.

INSTITUTION OF THE WORD OF GOD

When the gospel is given out, the emphasis is placed on the accuracy and the reliability and the importance of the Word of God.

> **For as the rain cometh down, and the snow from heaven, and returneth not thither, but watereth the earth, and maketh it bring forth and bud, that it may give seed to the sower, and bread to the eater.**

> **So shall my word be that goeth forth out of my mouth: it shall not return unto me void, but it shall accomplish that which I please, and it shall prosper in the thing whereto I sent it [Isa. 55:10–11].**

In this closing section there is a prominence given to the Word of God. The only place where the gospel is found is in the Word of God. Salvation is a revelation of God, and the Word of God is likened to the rain that comes down from heaven. You see, the gospel is not asking you to do something. Neither is the gospel something that man has thought up. Man does not work his way up to God by some Tower of Babel effort, but he receives God's revelation which comes down from heaven like rain. The rain causes the earth to become fruitful. The seeds germinate and fructify and bring forth abundantly. The Word of God is also the seed; and, when the rain and seed get together in the human heart, there will be fruit.

> **For ye shall go out with joy, and be led forth with peace: the mountains and the hills shall break forth before you into singing, and all the trees of the field shall clap their hands [Isa. 55:12].**

The rain causes the earth to respond with a green blanket of praise to God. During the Millennium the earth will respond with a note of praise to the Creator and Redeemer. "For we know that the whole creation groaneth and travaileth in pain together until now" (Rom. 8:22).

> **Instead of the thorn shall come up the fir tree, and instead of the brier shall come up the myrtle tree: and it shall be to the LORD for a name, for an everlasting sign that shall not be cut off [Isa. 55:13].**

This verse looks forward to the Millennium when the earth will be redeemed from the curse of sin. The curse of sin is expressed by the thorn and brier. When Christ died, He not only redeemed sinners, He also redeemed a sin-cursed earth.

CHAPTER 56

THEME: Grand particulars of the future Kingdom;
predicament of the present kingdom

The chapter before us follows a pattern that goes back to that marvelous fifty-third chapter, which tells of the salvation of the Lord provided for lost mankind by the sacrifice of His Son upon the Cross.

Now Isaiah the prophet returns to the nation of Israel and is speaking to his own people. What we have in this chapter is not a retreat to Mount Sinai (as some seem to think) but rather a victory march through the arch of triumph into the Millennium. It is a forward movement which is the logical outworking of what has preceded. It pertains particularly to Israel and radiates out into a widening circle of global benefits. This all rests on the new covenant which God has made with Israel. It will be the blessing for the earth in the future. At that time the Mosaic Law, which the Lord Jesus lifted to the nth degree in His Sermon on the Mount, will be enforced on the earth because Christ will be reigning. It will be His will and it will be His law.

The emphasis in this chapter is on ethics, not on events. The emphasis is on practice, not prophecy. All of this should influence our living today. The study of prophecy is not to entertain the curious or to intrigue the intellect but to encourage holy living. Remember that the apostle John wrote: "And every man that hath this hope in him purifieth himself, even as he is pure" (1 John 3:3). The study of prophecy gives us a purifying hope.

Isaiah now is looking forward into the Kingdom Age, the Millennium. The Lord Jesus is reigning. As we said, our Lord lifted the Mosaic Law to the nth degree in His Sermon on the Mount, which makes it absolutely impossible for anybody to be saved by keeping the Law. For instance, He said, ". . . Whosoever is angry with his brother without a cause shall be in danger of the judgment: and whosoever shall say to his brother, Raca [a word of contempt], shall be in danger of the council: but whosoever shall say, Thou fool, shall be in danger of hell fire" (Matt. 5:22). On that kind of basis, very few of us would escape. How, then, are we going to be saved? Well, we have a Savior who saves us. But when He is reigning on earth, there will be no hijacking of planes, no kidnapping, no murdering, no mugging. We will be able to walk in safety down Glory Boulevard and Hallelujah Avenue in Jerusalem; the earth will be a safe place in that day. Every man will dwell in peace under his own vine and fig tree, which means he is going to be a capitalist. Everyone will own property and will not be taxed for it. That's going to be great, isn't it!

GRAND PARTICULARS OF THE FUTURE KINGDOM

> **Thus saith the LORD, Keep ye judgment, and do justice: for my salvation is near to come, and my righteousness to be revealed [Isa. 56:1].**

"My salvation is near to come"—apparently the prophets expected the establishment of the Kingdom immediately. Although they made allowance for the possibility of an interval, they speak of it in the immediate future. "Salvation" is the *national* salvation of Israel. This is what was in the mind of the apostle Paul in Romans 11:26 when he said, "And so all Israel shall be saved: as it is written, There shall come out of Zion the Deliverer, and shall turn away ungodliness from Jacob." Anticipation of the coming salvation was to be an incentive to do justice—just as our hope of the coming of the Lord Jesus Christ is an incentive today to lead a holy life.

> **Blessed is the man that doeth this, and the son of man that layeth hold on it; that keepeth the sabbath from polluting it, and keepeth his hand from doing any evil [Isa. 56:2].**

This, you see, is for a people who are back under the Sabbath. The Sabbath will be restored to this earth during the Millennium. During this present day of grace we are definitely told: "Let no man therefore judge you in meat, or in drink, or in respect of an holyday, or of the new moon, or of the sabbath days" (Col. 2:16). Therefore, you and I are not under the Sabbath—which ought to be evident to everyone. But God intends to restore it to the earth when Christ reigns, for the law will go forth from Jerusalem.

> **Neither let the son of the stranger, that hath joined himself to the LORD, speak, saying, The LORD hath utterly separated me from his people: neither let the eunuch say, Behold, I am a dry tree [Isa. 56:3].**

The Gentile in that day is not to feel that he is an outsider because of God's peculiar arrangement with Israel. On the contrary, he is invited to step up and share the blessings. A eunuch could not serve as a priest under the Mosaic economy. In other words, a physical handicap will shut no one out in that future day.

> **For thus saith the LORD unto the eunuchs that keep my sabbaths, and choose the things that please me, and take hold of my covenant;**
>
> **Even unto them will I give in mine house and within my walls a place and a name better than of sons and of daughters: I will give them an everlasting name, that shall not be cut off [Isa. 56:4–5].**

The handicapped, the strangers, and all outcasts are invited to accept God's gracious overture of a position that is better than a son or daughter and a security that is everlasting. This the Law did not give. He is talking about the Millennium, of course.

> **Also the sons of the stranger, that join themselves to the LORD, to serve him, and to love the name of the LORD, to be his servants, every one that keepeth the sabbath from polluting it, and taketh hold of my covenant [Isa. 56:6].**

The stranger will be given a new heart that he might love the Lord in that day.

**Even them will I bring to my holy mountain, and make
them joyful in my house of prayer: their burnt offerings
and their sacrifices shall be accepted upon mine altar;
for mine house shall be called an house of prayer for all
people [Isa. 56:7].**

This is the verse from which the Lord quoted when He cleansed the
temple the second time. It was God's original intention that the temple
was to be for *all* people irrespective of their race, tongue, class, or
condition. It had long ceased to function as such in Christ's day.

Also the present-day church is as far removed from its primary
objective as the temple. The church has become like a suburban country club. It has moved from the downtown area and into the suburban
area where it is serving good meals and has good volleyball and bas-
ketball teams. But there are few personal workers bringing the lost to
the Lord.

**The Lord GOD which gathereth the outcasts of Israel
saith, Yet will I gather others to him, beside those that
are gathered unto him [Isa. 56:8].**

The Kingdom is to be worldwide in its extent and will include members of every family of the human race. God says in that day they are
going to go out after folk. I believe that the greatest time of turning to
Christ will take place during the Millennium.

PREDICAMENT OF THE PRESENT KINGDOM

Now that we have seen the marvelous view of the future Kingdom,
Isaiah returns to the predicament of the kingdom of his day. And we
see the same problems as we look around us today.

**All ye beasts of the field, come to devour, yea, all ye
beasts in the forest [Isa. 56:9].**

Our vision is now shifted from the lofty contemplation of the glorious
future Kingdom to the sorry condition of the then existing kingdom.

God was permitting the nations of the world to come in like wild and ferocious beasts, and they were robbing and pillaging His people. Assyria had already broken in, and Babylon was soon to break in; later others would come to plunder and destroy. If you have ever seen pictures of the walls of Jerusalem and the wailing wall, you can see that they are built of stones from different periods of civilizations. It is quite evident that the city has been destroyed repeatedly. History tells us that Jerusalem has been destroyed at least twenty-seven times, and today it is built upon debris. To go down to the place where Christ walked this earth you would have to dig thirty to fifty feet below the present surface. God permitted nations to come against Israel. Why? Because Israel failed Him so.

Note this remarkable verse—

His watchmen are blind: they are all ignorant, they are all dumb dogs, they cannot bark; sleeping, lying down, loving to slumber [Isa. 56:10].

This is a picture of the prophets and priests who spoke for God in that day. God permitted the enemy to take Jerusalem because of the weak and inadequate leaders of the people. They were blind. They were ignorant. They were dumb dogs. In the New Testament Paul warned the people to beware of dogs (see Phil. 3:2). What did he mean? Well, he's not talking about being wary of a stranger's dog that barks at you. He is referring to false teachers and preachers who are not declaring the full counsel of God. In Isaiah's day every shepherd had a dog to help him watch the sheep. The dog would lie down at night and keep one eye open. The minute a dangerous animal or a human being came to harm or to steal a sheep, the dog would bark. Watchmen—the prophets and the priests who should have been warning God's people and giving out the Word of God—were ignorant of it. They were like dumb dogs who did not bark when there was danger. It was easier for them to keep quiet.

Liberalism, in my judgment, came into being because of the cowardly position that many ministers took. When you preach the Word of God, you step on toes. I know this—I have been doing it for years. I try to be as nice as I can about preaching the Word, but it is strong and this verse is very strong. The man who stands in the pulpit and won't give out God's Word is a *dumb dog!* I didn't say that, but Isaiah did say it, and Isaiah wrote at the direction of the Holy Spirit of God. A dumb dog is a man who won't give out the Word of God. He lies down and sleeps. He cannot bark. He loves to slumber. It is much more comfortable for the pastor to try to please his people.

Over the years I have received many letters from pulpit committees asking me to recommend a pastor. Then they list the qualifications they want him to have. The top priority qualification is personality. They want a friendly pastor who knows how to communicate to all groups—a man that the senior citizens will love and the young people will love. Some of the letters don't even ask for a man with the ability to teach the Word of God! As a result, there are a lot of dumb dogs in pulpits. I am sorry to say this, but it is true, and Isaiah said it before I did.

Yea, they are greedy dogs which can never have enough, and they are shepherds that cannot understand: they all look to their own way, every one for his gain, from his quarter [Isa. 56:11].

"They are greedy dogs." They are concerned with their own personal interests rather than the welfare of their people.

One day I had lunch with a preacher friend of mine who is retired. He said to me, "McGee, you are making your message on the radio a little strong, aren't you? Suppose people turn against you and won't support your program?" I replied, "Then I'll go off the air and just tell the Lord about it. If He intends for me to stay on the air, He intends for me to give out His Word. Very frankly, I think that this is *His* problem, not mine. I'll just give out His word."

Come ye, say they, I will fetch wine, and we will fill ourselves with a strong drink; and to-morrow shall be as this day, and much more abundant [Isa. 56:12].

These people drowned their sad plight and condition in drink, and they faced the future as drunkards and blind optimists. There are many people today who are facing life like that. They drown their troubles in drink. In our nation today, my friend, we have an alcohol problem among adults and young people—and even children! I am seeing more drunkards today than I have ever seen before in my long life. When I was on a plane the other day, I was seated near a dear old grandmother. She was the sweetest looking little thing, and I just wished she were my grandmother. I was thinking, *Well, she is one person on this plane who won't be ordering a cocktail.* And, do you know, she ordered a Bloody Mary! Oh, boy, she tossed them down! Obviously she was accustomed to that sort of thing. The morality of our nation is gone, my friend. And a great many Christians don't want to hear about it; they would rather listen to soft, sweet music.

Well, you don't get into trouble when you play soft music, but you do when you give out the Word of God. But Isaiah told it like it was, and that's what I intend to do also.

CHAPTER 57

THEME: Contrast between the righteous and wicked;
comfort for the righteous; condemnation of the wicked

Now I grant you that today the wicked have it easy—they are the ones in *comfort*. They are the ones with the money, and they seem to be on top. But when we get to the end of the age, it will be comfort for the righteous and condemnation for the wicked.

This chapter marks the end of the second section of the final division of Isaiah, which I have labeled, "The salvation of Jehovah which comes through the suffering Servant." Those who come in humility and accept it are made righteous. Those who reject it proceed on their wicked way to judgment. This chapter brings us to the crossroads where the way that leads to life goes one way and the broad way to destruction goes another way. The destination and division are right here.

CONTRAST BETWEEN THE RIGHTEOUS AND WICKED

The righteous perisheth, and no man layeth it to heart: and merciful men are taken away, none considering that the righteous is taken away from evil to come [Isa. 57:1].

"The righteous perisheth." Many of God's wonderful saints are being taken away today through the doorway of death. God is removing them from a lot of trouble that is going to come in the future. When I started my ministry, I worried about myself. Then I had a child and I worried about her. Now I have two grandsons, and I worry about them. I no longer worry about myself or my daughter, but I do worry about those two little fellows because their lot in the future is going to be rough.

> **He shall enter into peace: they shall rest in their beds,**
> **each one walking in his uprightness [Isa. 57:2].**

"He shall enter into peace"—he shall have peace in his heart. "They shall rest in their beds, each one walking in his uprightness." If death comes to him while he is in bed, he will be removed from the Great Tribulation and will be taken into the presence of Christ. They will have peace regardless of what may come to them.

> **But draw near hither, ye sons of the sorceress, the seed**
> **of the adulterer and the whore [Isa. 57:3].**

Now God addresses the wicked. Even their ancestry is bad—note the label given their mothers!

> **Against whom do ye sport yourselves? against whom**
> **make ye a wide mouth, and draw out the tongue? are ye**
> **not children of transgression, a seed of falsehood [Isa.**
> **57:4].**

They have been the persecutors of the righteous. Up to this point God has not intervened. Look around you today. Attacks are being made upon the righteous. They are not having an easy time. The attacks are coming hard and fierce, and the wicked seem to get by with it.

> **Enflaming yourselves with idols under every green tree,**
> **slaying the children in the valleys under the clifts of the**
> **rocks? [Isa. 57:5].**

The wicked in the last days are the idolaters who have turned their backs on God. They are guilty of gross immorality and murder. Adultery and murder are two of the terrible sins of our day also—coupled with covetousness, which is idolatry. This is the condition of the wicked at the present time.

> **Among the smooth stones of the stream is thy portion;
> they, they are thy lot: even to them hast thou poured a
> drink offering, thou hast offered a meat offering. Should
> I receive comfort in these? [Isa. 57:6].**

They will even worship the smooth stones in the brook that once slew a giant. They worship everything except the living and true God.

> **Upon a lofty and high mountain hast thou set thy bed:
> even thither wentest thou up to offer sacrifice [Isa. 57:7].**

Now idolatry, associated with the groves on the mountaintops, gives place to scenes of the vilest immorality. It is a picture of the last days.

> **Behind the doors also and the posts hast thou set up thy
> remembrance: for thou hast discovered thyself to an-
> other than me, and art gone up; thou hast enlarged thy
> bed, and made thee a covenant with them; thou lovedst
> their bed where thou sawest it [Isa. 57:8].**

In the past, sin was committed in secret, but at the present time sin has become brazen and flaunts itself. Somebody asked me, "Don't you think there was as much immorality in the past as there is now?" I agreed that there may have been as much, but it was kept secret. Men were ashamed of their sin, but today they are not. The other day I listened to a pretty little girl on television talk about the man she lives with who is not her husband. She was commended by others on the program for not being a hypocrite. She may not be a hypocrite, but she is a sinner in God's sight. What would not even have been whispered about a few years ago is done in the open today. Sin has become a way of life. There are no longer high standards. The wheat and the tares are growing together exactly as the Lord said they would.

We see the contrast between the righteous and the wicked all through this section.

COMFORT FOR THE RIGHTEOUS

In the second division Isaiah speaks of comfort for the righteous.

> **For thus saith the high and lofty One that inhabiteth
> eternity, whose name is Holy; I dwell in the high and
> holy place, with him also that is of a contrite and hum-
> ble spirit, to revive the spirit of the humble, and to revive
> the heart of the contrite ones [Isa. 57:15].**

God in the last days comforts His own because of who He is—"the high and lofty One." He is the God of eternity. How feeble man is with his threescore years and ten down here. Man doesn't last very long on earth. The eternal God promises to take those who do not trust in themselves, but trust in Him, and He covers them as a mother hen covers her brood. What peace and security there is for those who belong to God! This verse looks beyond our day to the time of the Great Tribulation; we are coming here to the end of the age.

> **For I will not contend for ever, neither will I be always
> wroth: for the spirit should fail before me, and the souls
> which I have made [Isa. 57:16].**

He is the eternal God, but He will not always be angry with sin, because sin is to be removed.

> **For the iniquity of his covetousness was I wroth, and
> smote him: I hid me, and was wroth, and he went on
> forwardly in the way of his heart [Isa. 57:17].**

God explains why He punishes the wicked. The wicked are covetous, and they go on in rebellion against God. I am sure that any intelligent person knows that a holy God will one day stop rebellion. God will have to punish those with rebellious and proud hearts.

> **I have seen his ways, and will heal him: I will lead him
> also, and restore comforts unto him and to his mourners
> [Isa. 57:18].**

For those who will forsake the wickedness of their ways, He will heal and save them. He is a gracious God toward the righteous.

> **I create the fruit of the lips; Peace, peace to him that is
> far off, and to him that is near, saith the LORD; and I will
> heal him [Isa. 57:19].**

God alone can speak peace to the heart of the sinner.

CONDEMNATION OF THE WICKED

Each one of these last three divisions can be marked off at the place where God says, as He did in Isaiah 48:22, "There is no peace, saith the LORD, unto the wicked." I think this is something that is quite evident. Man's history is one of warfare and constant conflict. It is not only true among nations, but also between individuals—although they call it competition. You will find it in the business world, the social world, and in the religious world. You will find conflict in practically every town, every hamlet, and in many homes in our country. God says that there is no peace for the wicked. You cannot make peace in the human heart apart from God. So far no one has been able to do it.

> **But the wicked are like the troubled sea, when it cannot
> rest, whose waters cast up mire and dirt [Isa. 57:20].**

This is probably one of the most picturesque descriptions of the wicked in Scripture. Like the troubled and restless sea, the wicked person can find no rest or peace in his wicked ways. He continues on like a hunted criminal looking for deliverance and safety.

Several years ago an eighty-year-old man walked into the police station in Jackson, Mississippi, and said, "For fifty years I have been carrying a murder on my conscience. Another man has already paid the penalty for it, but I'm the one who is guilty. I *have* to make the confession of it." They found that, according to law, when another man had already paid the penalty, they couldn't execute the actual criminal or even hold him because another man had served the sentence. Probably the worst punishment this man had was fifty years of misery with a guilty conscience. He had had no peace of heart and mind at all.

There is no peace, saith my God, to the wicked [Isa. 57:21].

If the world can have peace today without God, then it is a contradiction of the Word of God. You cannot contradict God's Word. The wicked cannot have peace in the world, and they *don't* have it today. God says that the wicked will have no peace. That is an axiom of God, and it is like the law of gravity—it works.

CHAPTER 58

THEME: Exposure of Israel's wicked ways; explanation from God for rejecting religious acts; God's concern for their welfare

This chapter brings us to the final division of the prophecy of Isaiah—"The glory of Jehovah which comes through the suffering Servant." We move on in this section to the glory of the Kingdom. Inward wicked ways and outward religious forms delay the grace and glory of God and hurt the cause of Christ as much as anything. Men who are religious and are church members and yet curse like pagans, men who are dishonest in business, immoral in their social lives, yet talk about being good enough to meet God's standards, actually block the grace and glory of God.

The explanation is given here as to why the glory was withheld. The people were supercilious and cynical about their relationship to God. They were observing forms and dared to question the actions of God toward them. They sat in judgment upon God and His methods. A lot of people still do this today. In spite of their outward observance of religion they indulge in their own wicked ways.

This same spirit was manifested after the Babylonian captivity, which reveals that the captivity did not cure them. In Malachi 3:13–14 we read, "Your words have been stout against me, saith the Lord. Yet ye say, What have we spoken so much against thee? Ye have said, It is vain to serve God: and what profit is it that we have kept his ordinance, and that we have walked mournfully before the Lord of hosts?" They were criticizing God for not blessing them—yet look how religious they were! They went to the temple and they made sacrifices. It was brazen effrontery and audacity to question God! This is the spirit of the natural man with his outward show of religion. His heart is far from God, and his way is wicked. The veneer of godliness is nauseating to the Lord Jesus Christ. The Lord said to the Laodicean church, "So then because thou art lukewarm, and neither cold nor hot, I will spue thee out of my mouth" (Rev. 3:16). This is the attitude of the Lord Jesus to a lot of churchianity in our day.

EXPOSURE OF ISRAEL'S WICKED WAYS

Cry aloud, spare not, lift up thy voice like a trumpet, and shew my people their transgression, and the house of Jacob their sins [Isa. 58:1].

The prophet is commanded to cry aloud a message that is always unpopular, which is to point out the transgressions and sins of a people who think they are very religious. This will bring down the bitter displeasure and caustic invective upon one's head. Only a very brave man will do it. I would say that the basic weakness of liberalism in the pulpit is its aim to please the natural man without telling him the real truth about his fatal disease. The medical profession today would be guilty of gross negligence if they followed the same procedure with the physical part of man that religion plays with the spiritual part of man. When the doctor told me I had cancer, I tried my best to get him to say that it was something else. He said, "I am going to tell you exactly what is wrong with you. I will tell it exactly like it is. If I don't, you won't have any confidence in me." God is telling it exactly like it is. And He wants His servants to tell mankind that they are suffering from the fatal disease of sin, which is going to eventuate in *eternal death,* eternal separation from almighty God.

Yet they seek me daily, and delight to know my ways, as a nation that did righteousness, and forsook not the ordinance of their God: they ask of me the ordinances of justice; they take delight in approaching to God [Isa. 58:2].

I think there is an element of God's biting satire in this statement. These people were attending the temple worship regularly. They were going through the ordinances punctiliously. They were meticulous in following the forms of worship. They actually *enjoyed* going to the temple; yet their lives bore no resemblance to those of believers. What was true in that day is also true today.

> **Wherefore have we fasted, say they, and thou seest not? wherefore have we afflicted our soul, and thou takest no knowledge? Behold, in the day of your fast ye find pleasure, and exact all your labours [Isa. 58:3].**

These people are petulantly complaining. They ask the reason for fasting and self-infliction if God doesn't take note of it and pat them on the back for the ritual. Yet their hearts are far from God. They evidently had made fasting an important part of their religion. God never gave them fast days; He gave them feast days. It is true that they were to afflict their souls in connection with the great Day of Atonement, and in times of sin they were to fast. Fasting was the outward expression of the soul, but they had made it a form which ministered to their ego and pride. They *boasted* of the fact that they fasted. Fasting was to be a private matter between the soul and God—not a public show. Our Lord condemned them for abusing the fast. When He was here He said, "Moreover when ye fast, be not, as the hypocrites, of a sad countenance: for they disfigure their faces, that they may appear unto men to fast. Verily I say unto you, They have their reward [which was to be seen of men]" (Matt. 6:16). They needn't expect anything from God, for they didn't do it because of their relationship with Him. The Lord Jesus said to those who are His own: "But thou, when thou fastest, anoint thine head, and wash thy face; that thou appear not unto men to fast, but unto thy Father which is in secret: and thy Father, which seeth in secret, shall reward thee openly" (Matt. 6:17–18). Real religion is a personal relationship with Christ, and it is as secret and private as anything can possibly be. Do you go around and tell others about your intimate relationship with your wife or your husband? Of course you don't. My friend, if you have a personal relationship with Jesus Christ, it is a precious secret between the two of you. You witness for Him, but you don't reveal your intimate moments with Him. My friend, are you boasting about your religion, or about going through a certain ceremony or ritual? Shame on you! They are nothing in the sight of God—unless they reveal what is within your heart. Oh, how we need reality rather than ritual!

I am of the opinion that many folk in that day questioned Isaiah's message. They probably said, "Isaiah, what in the world are you talking about? You criticize these people who are very religious, who go regularly to the temple and make their sacrifices!" But, you see, God knows the heart. Their religion was only superficial. They had no real relationship with God.

EXPLANATION FROM GOD FOR
REJECTING RELIGIOUS ACTS

In this next section God explains His reason for rejecting their show of religion.

> **Behold, ye fast for strife and debate, and to smite with the fist of wickedness: ye shall not fast as ye do this day, to make your voice to be heard on high [Isa. 58:4].**

God explains why He cannot accept their fasting. They thought it gave them special acceptance with Him.

> **Is it such a fast that I have chosen? a day for a man to afflict his soul? is it to bow down his head as a bulrush, and to spread sackcloth and ashes under him? wilt thou call this a fast, and an acceptable day to the LORD? [Isa. 58:5].**

God had not commanded their fasting, and their acts of worship were entirely outward and did not reveal the condition of the heart.

This is largely the condition of the contemporary church. I don't say it is the condition of your church—there are many wonderful churches. But, by and large, the organized church has only a form of godliness.

> Is not this the fast that I have chosen? to loose the bands
> of wickedness, to undo the heavy burdens, and to let the
> oppressed go free, and that ye break every yoke? [Isa.
> 58:6].

This is tremendous—it gets right down to the nitty-gritty, right down where the rubber meets the road. God says in effect, "If you really want to fast, let Me tell you what to do: Instead of fasting and going around with a pious look, stop your sinning. Stop your gossiping. Stop the things that reveal the wickedness and the evil in your hearts. Demonstrate your faith in Me by your conduct. Start being honest in your dealings. Be truthful in what you say. Instead of seeing you in sackcloth and covered with ashes, I'd like to see you clean on the inside."

My friend, I am of the opinion that the Lord could stop many church services today and say, "Listen, let's cut this out. Why are you going through this form? You are not getting close to me. You are not pleasing Me. When you leave this service, you gossip, you have bitterness in your heart, you are not moral in your conduct, and you are living loose lives. You think you are pleasing Me by your religious form. I want you to know that you are not pleasing Me. That is the reason I am rejecting you."

> Is it not to deal thy bread to the hungry, and that thou
> bring the poor that are cast out to thy house? when thou
> seest the naked, that thou cover him; and that thou hide
> not thyself from thine own flesh? [Isa. 58:7].

They were turning their backs on the poor and needy. They even refused to show kindness and love to their own flesh and blood. Their religion was as cold as the north side of a tombstone in January! They didn't have a heart for God. When you have a heart for God, my friend, you will also have a heart for other folk. You will want to be helpful to them and be a blessing to them. You cannot be hateful and fundamental in your theology at the same time. All of the criticism and unloveliness today is harmful to the cause of Christ. Isaiah has a tremendous message for us!

God told His people that He didn't want their so-called worship—they were just going through a form. They were just "playing church." He told them that they might think they were having fun, but it was going to become a burden to them because they would become weary trying to keep up a front before the world. God said to them, "Come clean. Demonstrate in your lives that you have reality."

Do you see why Isaiah is not popular? You will never find liberalism dealing with this part of the Bible. They like to turn to the Sermon on the Mount and pick out a few verses, such as: "Blessed are the merciful: for they shall obtain mercy" (Matt. 5:7). That is great, but the important thing is to confess your sin to God and allow Christ to live His life through you. Religion is a great cover-up today. Oh, how we need a personal relationship with Christ!

GOD'S CONCERN FOR THEIR WELFARE

God wants His people to turn to Him in a real way.

> **Then shall thy light break forth as the morning, and thine health shall spring forth speedily: and thy righteousness shall go before thee; the glory of the LORD shall be thy reward [Isa. 58:8].**

God could not manifest His blessing and glory to a people who practiced their religion so badly. This is one of the reasons the world today is not convinced that God is in His holy temple. The world is passing by the church. Why? They don't believe God is there. And I suspect they might be right. God says here, "I can't manifest myself because of your lives." How many of us are blocking the way! The story is told that when Alexander the Great returned from one of his campaigns, he rushed to find his old teacher, Aristotle, the great Greek philosopher. It so happened that Aristotle was taking a bath when his visitor arrived. Alexander told him about his campaign and then said, "Now what can I do for you?" The old philosopher was not at all impressed with this young upstart and continued his bathing. Alexander repeated the question, "Now what can I do for you?" Finally old Aristotle replied, "Well, you can get out of my light!" Perhaps we are saying to God, "What can I do for You?" I think God would answer, "You can get out of my light!" Let's allow His light to shine through us. That's the important thing.

> **Then shalt thou call, and the LORD shall answer; thou shalt cry, and he shall say, Here I am. If thou take away from the midst of thee the yoke, the putting forth of the finger, and speaking vanity [Isa. 58:9].**

God *wanted* to hear their prayers and He *wanted* to bless. He wanted to open the windows of heaven and pour out a blessing upon them, but their hearts weren't open to receive it. We say, "Our prayers are not answered." Why? Is it because God does not want to answer them? No! The problem is that our hearts are not open to receive the blessing God really wants to give us. God says, "The minute you cry to Me, here I am."

When I was a boy, I had typhoid fever and double pneumonia at the same time. I lived in a little country town, and one night the country doctor thought I was going to die. My mother sat by my bed all night. I was delirious most of the time, but I can still remember coming out of it and calling her name, "Mama?" She would say, "Here I am." What a comfort that was for a little boy. And today what a comfort to know that when we go to God in prayer, He is there. He says, "Here I am." In effect, God says, "It's up to you from now on. If you come in the name of My Son, make a request that is in My will, and your heart is right, I'm going to move right along with you." When we have prayers which are not being answered, the problem is with us.

> **And if thou draw out thy soul to the hungry, and satisfy the afflicted soul; then shall thy light rise in obscurity, and thy darkness be as the noon day [Isa. 58:10].**

God asked them to practice one specific thing that He might bless them. He only picked out one thing. He could have picked out a dozen things, but He chose only one. God *promised* to bless them if they would show reality in their religion.

> **And the LORD shall guide thee continually, and satisfy thy soul in drought, and make fat thy bones: and thou shalt be like a watered garden, and like a spring of water, whose waters fail not [Isa. 58:11].**

God wanted to bless them, you see.

> **If thou turn away thy foot from the sabbath, from doing thy pleasure on my holy day; and call the sabbath a delight, the holy of the LORD, honourable; and shall honor him, not doing thine own ways, or finding thine own pleasure, nor speaking thine own words [Isa. 58:13].**

God gave the Sabbath to the nation Israel. God said, "It is a sign between me and the children of Israel for ever . . ." (Exod. 31:17). For something interesting, read the entire passage of Exodus 31:12–18. Now God turns to this specific thing that He commanded them as a people.

For us today it is a little different. We are told: "Let us therefore fear, lest, a promise being left us of entering into his rest, any of you should seem to come short of it" (Heb. 4:1). The word for "rest" is *sabbath*—we should not come short of entering into His rest. "For he that is entered into his rest [that is, the sabbath], he also hath ceased from his own works, as God did from his" (Heb. 4:10). Now have you entered into His sabbath, which is the rest of redemption? Have you come to the place where you completely, fully trust Christ—that He has done everything necessary for your salvation and you are resting in His finished work? Or do you feel compelled to *do* something in order to earn or not lose your salvation? My friend, He wants us to fully trust Christ. To enter into His rest will mean not only great bless-

ing for us, but it will open up an avenue of service for us. The thing
that brought the apostle Paul to a life of missionary activity was to
enter into the rest of redemption.

> **Then shalt thou delight thyself in the LORD; and I will
> cause thee to ride upon the high places of the earth, and
> feed thee with the heritage of Jacob thy father: for the
> mouth of the LORD hath spoken it [Isa. 58:14].**

The horizon here is extended, and the vista of the future opens before
us. They may delay the approaching glory, but they cannot destroy
God's plan for the coming manifestation of His glory.

CHAPTER 59

THEME: Condemnation of Israel; confession of Israel; coming of the Redeemer to Israel

This remarkable chapter continues God's charges against Israel, and He spells them out. Their sins had brought about their sad state. Religion had become a cover-up for their sins. God refuses to hear because of their iniquities, not because He was hard of hearing. Many people today think God has a hearing problem. God hears us all right. The problem lies with us.

Their sins are referred to thirty-two times. Many words are used to describe their sins: iniquities, sins, defiled with blood, lies, perverseness, vanity, mischief, adder's eggs, spider's web, viper, works, violence, evil, wasting, destruction, crooked paths, darkness, transgressions, departing, oppression, revolt, conceiving, and uttering of falsehood. There are twenty-three separate charges brought against them. What a picture this is! For Israel there will be a time of national confession of sin. In that day there shall be a great mourning in Jerusalem. We are told about it in Zechariah 12:11–14: "In that day shall there be a great mourning in Jerusalem, as the mourning of Hadadrimmon in the valley of Megiddon. And the land shall mourn, every family apart; the family of the house of Nathan apart, and their wives apart; the family of the house of Levi apart, and their wives apart; the family of Shimei apart, and their wives apart; all the families that remain, every family apart, and their wives apart."

CONDEMNATION OF ISRAEL

Behold, the LORD's hand is not shortened, that it cannot save; neither his ear heavy, that it cannot hear [Isa. 59:1].

The reason that Israel was not saved in Isaiah's day was not due to any weakness in the "mighty bared arm of Jehovah" which we saw in

Isaiah 53. The Lord's hand was not shortened. Neither was it due to any faulty connection in His communication with man. Likewise in our day it is not the mental hurdles that man has to surmount nor any of his many problems, but his sin separates him from God.

> **But your iniquities have separated between you and your God, and your sins have hid his face from you, that he will not hear [Isa. 59:2].**

Let me quote the comment of Alexander Maclaren in *The Books of Isaiah and Jeremiah:* "It is not because God is great and I am small, it is not because He lives for ever, and my life is but a hand-breadth, it is not because of the difference between His omniscience and my ignorance, His strength and my weakness, that I am parted from Him: 'Your sins have separated between you and your God.' And no man, build he Babels ever so high, can reach thither. There is one means by which the separation is at an end, and by which all objective hindrances to union, and all subjective hindrances, are alike swept away. Christ has come, and in Him the heavens have bended down to touch, and touching to bless this low earth, and man and God are at one once more."

Now throughout this first section God spells out their sins. It is rather a discouraging picture of the human family—and of you and me. Then we have a confession of Israel, which is coming in the future when the Redeemer comes to Zion.

CONFESSION OF ISRAEL

> **Therefore is judgment far from us, neither doth justice overtake us: we wait for light, but behold obscurity; for brightness but we walk in darkness [Isa. 59:9].**

The change of pronouns here indicates that there is another speaker. Instead of "your" and "their," it is "we" and "our" and "us" now. This is Israel's confession. They confess they are in darkness. They confess that their religious rituals have all been a pretense.

Many folk need to do this in our day. I played golf with a dentist and a broker some time ago in Tulsa, Oklahoma. Both of these men told me how they came to know the Lord. Both of them had been members in rich liberal churches. They were both wealthy men. One of the men told me that one day he simply got tired of being a hypocrite, so he went to the Lord and confessed that he was a hypocrite and wanted reality. He accepted Jesus Christ as his Savior. Oh, how this is needed today! It could actually bring revival to our churches.

Now notice Israel's confession:

> **We grope for the wall like the blind, and we grope as if we had no eyes: we stumble at noon day as in the night; we are in desolate places as dead men [Isa. 59:10].**

You see, they are in darkness. What a picture of the man who does not have a personal relationship with God!

But when Israel will make this confession—and they *will* make it in the future—to these specific charges, they also will repudiate their sins. My friend, our confessions to God should be specific and then the sins repudiated. Each sin should be confessed privately to God.

I have no heart to go through this list of Israel's sins—I have problems enough with my own.

COMING OF THE REDEEMER TO ISRAEL

Notice that the pronoun changes again. The Redeemer will come to Zion.

> **And the Redeemer shall come to Zion, and unto them that turn from transgression in Jacob, saith the Lord [Isa. 59:20].**

Many people ask, "Will the whole nation be saved?" No, "For they are not all Israel, which are of Israel" (Rom. 9:6). Those saved will only be a remnant. And there appears to be only a remnant in the church who are actually saved.

But the Redeemer is coming some day to Zion, and at that time there will be a great confession of sin. Zechariah 12:10 tells us about it: "And I will pour upon the house of David, and upon the inhabitants of Jerusalem, the spirit of grace and of supplications: and they shall look upon me whom they have pierced, and they shall mourn for him, as one mourneth for his only son, and shall be in bitterness for him, as one that is in bitterness for his firstborn."

As for me, this is my covenant with them, saith the Lord; My spirit that is upon thee, and my words which I have put in thy mouth, shall not depart out of thy mouth, nor out of the mouth of thy seed, nor out of the mouth of thy seed's seed, saith the Lord, from henceforth and for ever [Isa. 59:21].

God has made a covenant that the Redeemer is coming to Zion. There will never be a time when this promise will be entirely forsaken, for this is God's purpose. It *will* be fulfilled in His good time.

CHAPTER 60

THEME: The Redeemer and Gentiles come to Jerusalem; the return of Israel to Jerusalem; Jerusalem's realization of all God's promises

The last part of Isaiah, I have a notion, is virgin territory to a great many folks because no school of prophecy dwells on this particular section of Scripture. In this chapter we see the Sun of Righteousness rising upon Israel; it is that which Malachi said would come to pass in the last days. When He comes, it will be like the sun rising into midnight darkness. In that day the nation Israel will reflect the glory light here upon the entire earth. The church, in the meantime, has gone to be with Christ. To attempt to make the nation Israel and the church synonymous is an interpretation that bogs down when you get into an area like this. It is an unsatisfactory interpretation which does not meet the dimensions of these prophecies. I emphasize this because it has caused so much confusion. Certain schools of Bible interpretation place little importance on prophecy because they neglect sections like this great chapter in the Word of God.

This third and final division of the Book of Isaiah presents the Redeemer on the Cross (ch. 53). Following that there has been a definite progress and development which speaks not of the *government* of God (as the first part of Isaiah did), but rather of the *grace* of God. In the first section the emphasis was upon *law;* here it is upon *grace.* We find here—as we found also in the first section—that there is *love* in law. Also in this section we find that there is *law* in love.

The chapter before us brings us to the full manifestation of the Millennium. Chapter 59 closed by saying that the Redeemer will come to Zion. Now as we move along in chapter 60, He has come. In the Hebrew language there is what is known as the prophetic tense—when the prophet goes beyond the event and looks back at it as if it were history. Isaiah speaks of many future things as having already taken place. For example, he begins by saying, "Arise, shine; for thy light is come, and the glory of the Lord *is* risen upon thee." And you can understand that for God to say a thing is going to happen, He is already on the other side of it—for Him it is just the same as its having taken place. In other words, prophecy is the mold into which history is poured.

THE REDEEMER AND GENTILES COME TO JERUSALEM

Arise, shine; for thy light is come, and the glory of the Lord is risen upon thee [Isa. 60:1].

The Light has now come of which Malachi had spoken: "But unto you that fear my name shall the Sun of righteousness arise with healing in his wings . . ." (Mal. 4:2).

For, behold, the darkness shall cover the earth, and gross darkness the people: but the Lord shall arise upon thee, and his glory shall be seen upon thee [Isa. 60:2].

The Lord Jesus Christ is the Light of the world—that was one of His claims when He was here. When He comes to the earth the second time, He is that Light.

"For, behold, the darkness shall cover the earth." The coming of the Light is necessitated by the night of spiritual darkness that has covered the earth—and covers the earth today. In spite of the preaching of the gospel for nineteen hundred years, there is a wider circle of darkness today than ever before. Light *must* precede the future blessings. The Sun of Righteousness *must* rise to bring the millennial day. The preaching of the gospel was never intended by God to bring in the Millennium because it takes the Light to bring in the Millennium. And who is the Light? The Lord Jesus. We need the presence of the Redeemer in Zion, and He is going to bring the Gentiles from afar.

And the Gentiles shall come to thy light, and kings to the brightness of thy rising [Isa. 60:3].

I believe that the greatest revival—that is, the greatest turning to God is yet in the future. In Romans 11:15 Paul says, "For if the casting away of them [Israel] be the reconciling of the world, what shall the receiving of them be, but life from the dead?" It will be the resurrection of the nation Israel and the resurrection of the world. You and I live on a little clod of earth in space that is just a glorified cemetery!

> **Lift up thine eyes round about, and see: all they gather themselves together, they come to thee: thy sons shall come from far, and thy daughters shall be nursed at thy side [Isa. 60:4].**

Rebellious and scattered, they are going to come back to the Land of Promise—but in obedience to God. The women, who are weaker than men, are carried, like women in the East often carry their children, on their hips.

> **Then thou shalt see, and flow together, and thine heart shall fear, and be enlarged; because the abundance of the sea shall be converted unto thee, the forces of the Gentiles shall come unto thee [Isa. 60:5].**

Here you see the tremendous movement of all peoples toward Jerusalem—by land, by sea, and by air—which will be an occasion of astonishment.

> **The multitude of camels shall cover thee, the dromedaries of Midian and Ephah, all they from Sheba shall come: they shall bring gold and incense; and they shall shew forth the praises of the LORD [Isa. 60:6].**

Again wise men, not only from the East, but from all over the world, will come with gifts of gold and incense for the Redeemer. Notice that they are not going to bring myrrh. Why? Because myrrh spoke of Christ's death at His first coming. At His second coming they bring no myrrh. This is a remarkable verse!

All the flocks of Kedar shall be gathered together unto thee, the rams of Nebaioth shall minister unto thee: they shall come up with acceptance on mine altar, and I will glorify the house of my glory [Isa. 60:7].

Flocks are brought to Jerusalem for sacrifice. The sacrifices will be reinstituted in the millennial temple. This may be difficult for some to accept, but the Old Testament is very definite at this point. Read, for example, Ezekiel 40—44. These sacrifices, I believe, will point back to the death of Christ as in the Old Testament they pointed forward to His death. They will have the same meaning.

THE RETURN OF ISRAEL TO JERUSALEM

Who are these that fly as a cloud, and as the doves to their windows? [Isa. 60:8].

If there is any prophecy in Scripture that suggests the airplane, this is it, but I think the direct reference is to ships of the sea. It does not refer to what is happening today, although I understand that Jews who have come from farther East than Israel thought this prophecy was being fulfilled as they were brought by American airplanes to the land of Israel; but it does not quite meet the dimensions of the prophecy.

Surely the isles shall wait for me, and the ships of Tarshish first, to bring thy sons from far, their silver and their gold with them, unto the name of the LORD thy God, and to the Holy One of Israel, because he hath glorified thee [Isa. 60:9].

"Tarshish," as used here, evidently refers to all seagoing nations whose ships will be used to return Israel to the Land of Promise. The nations who once destroyed Israel will assist in her recovery. At that time Russia will send the Jews back to their land. Instead of demanding payment, they will send the Jews off with gifts as the Egyptians did. After all, Israel only collected their back pay from the Egyptians, and they had a great deal coming because they had been in slavery for four hundred years.

> **Therefore thy gates shall be open continually; they shall not be shut day nor night; that men may bring unto thee the forces of the Gentiles, and that their kings may be brought [Isa. 60:11].**

The nations of the world that are saved are going to come to Jerusalem in the Millennium.

> **For the nation and kingdom that will not serve thee shall perish; yea, those nations shall be utterly wasted [Isa. 60:12].**

The Lord Jesus made it clear that His judgment upon the nations would be based on their treatment of the Jews (See Matt. 25:31–46).

In the Millennium every knee shall bow and every tongue shall confess that Jesus Christ is Lord (see Phil. 2:10–11). In the Millennium all mankind will be forced to bow to Jesus. The force, of course, will be the force of public opinion in that day. In their hearts there will be those who won't want to bow, but they will go through the motions. Then when Satan is released at the end of the Millennium, those with rebellious hearts will naturally gravitate toward him, which will be the last rebellion. Then the eternal aspect of the Kingdom will be introduced. I believe at that time certain radical changes will take place. It won't be a patched-up earth, but a new earth and new heavens will come into existence. God is going to make all things new, and He is going to let me start over again. I am looking forward to that! I haven't done so well since I began my life in Texas many years ago. I would like to start over. God is going to make all things new. He is not going to retool the old nature; He is going to give me a new nature, and He is going to give a new nature to everyone who has trusted in Him. What a glorious, wonderful day that will be!

JERUSALEM'S REALIZATION
OF ALL GOD'S PROMISES

Whereas thou hast been forsaken and hated, so that no man went through thee, I will make thee an eternal excellency, a joy of many generations [Isa. 60:15].

As Isaiah said in chapter 2, Jerusalem will become the center of the earth. A great deal of blessing will come in that day.

Thou shalt also suck the milk of the Gentiles, and shalt suck the breast of kings: and thou shalt know that I the Lord am thy Saviour and thy Redeemer, the mighty One of Jacob [Isa. 60:16].

The riches of Jerusalem, which were taken away by the nations, will be restored with interest.

For brass I will bring gold, and for iron I will bring silver, and for wood brass, and for stones iron: I will also make thy officers peace, and thine exactors righteousness [Isa. 60:17].

It is interesting that we see so many objects of brass in that land today. The markets of Egypt and Lebanon sell many brass objects, but in that future day they will be replaced by silver and gold objects for sale. In other words, precious metals will become commonplace again. Now notice some other wonderful things which will take place:

The sun shall be no more thy light by day; neither for brightness shall the moon give light unto thee: but the Lord shall be unto thee an everlasting light, and thy God thy glory.

Thy sun shall no more go down; neither shall thy moon withdraw itself: for the Lord shall be thine everlasting light, and the days of thy mourning shall be ended [Isa. 60:19–20].

Jesus, the Light of the world, will be there. He is also the Light of the New Jerusalem. The universe no longer will need street lights on the corners. After all, the suns and stars are street lights out in space. God did not light up the universe very well because sin had come in, but in that day He is really going to light things up!

> **A little one shall become a thousand, and a small one a strong nation: I the LORD will hasten it in his time [Isa. 60:22].**

Human strength will be increased in that day without resorting to vitamins! The Lord Jesus called attention to the fact that the spirit is willing but the flesh is weak. In my own experience I find that my flesh just doesn't keep up with me! I would like to go much faster, but my body holds me back. However, in that future day all of this will be corrected—corrected here on earth as it will be corrected for the heavenly people.

CHAPTER 61

THEME: *Distinction between the first and second comings of Christ; delights of the Millennium*

This chapter is of peculiar interest in view of the fact that the Lord Jesus opened His public ministry in Nazareth by quoting from it. This chapter continues the full blessings of the Millennium with Israel as the center of all earthly benefits. The last section projects us into the total benefits of the Millennium.

DISTINCTION BETWEEN THE FIRST AND SECOND COMINGS OF CHRIST

Here in the first three verses we have one of the most remarkable passages of scripture, and it helps us to correctly interpret the Bible.

> **The spirit of the Lord God is upon me; because the Lord hath anointed me to preach good tidings unto the meek; he hath sent me to bind up the brokenhearted, to proclaim liberty to the captives, and the opening of the prison to them that are bound;**
>
> **To proclaim the acceptable year of the Lord, and the day of vengeance of our God; to comfort all that mourn [Isa. 61:1–2].**

Now here we are given a system of biblical interpretation. If I were to read this without knowing the New Testament, I would not be sure about whom he is talking. Who is it who says, "The spirit of the Lord God is upon me"? If He is the Lord Jesus, does it refer to His first or second coming? Well, in the New Testament we have God's interpretation. When the Lord Jesus went into the synagogue in His hometown of Nazareth, He read this section: "And he came to Nazareth, where he had been brought up: and, as his custom was, he went into the synagogue on the sabbath day, and stood up for to read. And there was delivered unto him the book of the prophet Esaias. And when he had opened the book, he found the place where it was written, The Spirit of the Lord is upon me, because he hath anointed me to preach the gospel to the poor; he hath sent me to heal the brokenhearted, to preach deliverance to the captives, and recovering of sight to the blind, to set at liberty them that are bruised. To preach the acceptable year of the Lord" (Luke 4:16–19). Now, my friend, if you will look again at Isaiah 61:1–2, you will see that He is not even through the sentence. Why didn't He keep reading? The rest of the sentence is "and the day of vengeance of our God"—why didn't He preach that? Notice this: He *closed* the book. That was a deliberate action. "And he closed the book, and he gave it again to the minister, and sat down. And the eyes of all them that were in the synagogue were fastened on him. And he began to say unto them, This day is this scripture fulfilled in your ears" (Luke 4:20–21). Isaiah's prophecy up to that point was fulfilled by Christ's first coming. Isaiah had not made the distinction between the first and second comings of Christ, but the Lord Jesus made the distinction. In Isaiah's prophecy a little "and" separates the first and second comings of Christ. You might say that this little *and* is more than nineteen hundred years long! The prophets wrote of the first and second comings of Christ; they saw these two great events, but they did not know the length of time that lay between them. The apostle Peter confirms this: "Of which salvation the prophets have inquired and searched diligently, who prophesied of the grace that should come unto you: searching what, or what manner of time the Spirit of Christ which was in them did signify, when it testified beforehand the sufferings of Christ, and the glory that should follow" (1 Pet. 1:10–11). Peter says that the prophets spoke of the sufferings of Christ and the glory of Christ—we see this in both the first and second sections of Isaiah.

Let me illustrate the problem the prophets had as they looked into the future. Behind my home in Pasadena, California—several miles from the foothills—looms Mount Wilson upon which Mount Wilson Observatory and the antennas of several radio stations are situated. Behind Mount Wilson I can see another mountain, Mount Waterman.

It looks as if the two mountains are right there together, but I've been up in those mountains and I know there are at least twenty-five miles between them. It is impossible to see that distance between them unless you are there.

Now the prophet was way down in the valley looking into the future. He saw the first and second comings of Christ. Perhaps Isaiah was a little confused. In one breath how could he say that the Lord was going to bind up the brokenhearted, and open the prisons, and at the same time announce the day of the vengeance of our God? How can both be true? If the prophet had stood where we stand today, he would have understood. We are in the valley between the first and second comings of Christ. We can look back to the first coming when He came to fulfill Luke 4:20–21 and to die on the cross as our Redeemer, as we saw in Isaiah 53. Somewhere beyond that mountain peak is the next one, the second coming of Christ. Before He comes again, however, the church will be removed form the earthly scene. In John 14:3 Jesus said, "And if I go and prepare a place for you, I will come again, and receive you unto myself; that where I am, there ye may be also."

"To proclaim the acceptable year of the LORD, and the day of vengeance of our God." When He comes to earth the second time to establish His Kingdom, it will be with vengeance. We will see that in chapter 63 where He is treading the winepress of the wrath of God. It is not a pretty scene—God didn't say it would be pretty. But Christ is going to put down the rebellion that is here on this earth. You see, this little earth is still under His control. Emerson was wrong when he said that *things* are in the saddle and ride mankind. The Lord Jesus Christ is in the saddle, and He is in control. He is the King, and He is coming some day to put down all rebellion; that will be "the day of vengeance of our God."

"To comfort all that mourn." Immediately after announcing the day of vengeance, He says He is going to comfort all that mourn—those who mourn over their sin, who long in their hearts for a better day, and who want to be obedient unto Him.

Not only will He comfort *all* who mourn but all that mourn in Zion—

> To appoint unto them that mourn in Zion, to give unto
> them beauty for ashes, the oil of joy for mourning, the
> garment of praise for the spirit of heaviness; that they
> might be called trees of righteousness, the planting of
> the LORD, that he might be glorified [Isa. 61:3].

I believe that Isaiah knew his geography, and when he said "Zion," he
meant Zion—not Los Angeles, Salt Lake City, Florida, or South America. Zion, the highest spot in Jerusalem, was well known to Isaiah.

Now, speaking specifically of the Jews, he says, "to give unto them
beauty for ashes, the oil of joy for mourning, the garment of praise for
the spirit of heaviness; that they might be called trees of righteousness, the planting of the LORD, that he might be glorified." You can see
that beyond the "day of vengeance," which will be amplified in chapter 63, is the peace and the prosperity of the Millennium.

Isaiah makes a play upon words with "beauty" and "ashes"—it is
like saying in English that God will exchange joy for judgment or a
song for a sigh. After the sighing and the judgment there will be joy
and singing.

> And they shall build the old wastes, they shall raise up
> the former desolations, and they shall repair the waste
> cities, the desolations of many generations [Isa. 61:4].

The land of Israel has yet to receive this facelift, which will restore its
Edenic beauty. What is happening in our day in Israel is wonderful. It
has caused Dr. W. F. Albright, a great Hebrew scholar, to take the position that he now believes in prophecy—since a nation that has been
out of their land for twenty-five hundred years is back in their land. It
apparently has made a believer out of him. But let us be very careful
not to call it the fulfillment of *this* prophecy. The "facelift" that this
verse is talking about will take place at the beginning of the Millennium, and we are not at that place in time right now.

> And strangers shall stand and feed your flocks, and the
> sons of the alien shall be your plowmen and your vine-
> dressers [Isa. 61:5].

This is a real picture of prosperity.

> **But ye shall be named the Priests of the LORD: men shall call you the Ministers of our God: ye shall eat the riches of the Gentiles, and in their glory shall ye boast yourselves [Isa. 61:6].**

"Men shall call you the Ministers of our God." Israel is going to be a priesthood of believers during the Millennium. It was God's original intention that the entire nation would be priests. In Exodus 19:6 God said of Israel, "And ye shall be unto me a kingdom of priests, and an holy nation. These are the words which thou shalt speak unto the children of Israel." Because of their sin this was never attained, but it will be attained in the Millennium.

> **For your shame ye shall have double; and for confusion they shall rejoice in their portion: therefore in their land they shall possess the double: everlasting joy shall be unto them [Isa. 61:7].**

In other words, everlasting joy shall be Israel's portion. It will be fullness of joy! What a great day that will be.

> **For I the LORD love judgment, I hate robbery for burnt offering; and I will direct their work in truth, and I will make an everlasting covenant with them [Isa. 61:8].**

Their lives then will *adorn* their religious ritual. We have looked at several passages which spoke of the fact that Israel went through all of the rituals, but God condemned her for it because her heart was not in it. Things will be changed in that future day.

> **And their seed shall be known among the Gentiles, and their offspring among the people: all that see them shall acknowledge them, that they are the seed which the LORD hath blessed [Isa. 61:9].**

Anti-Semitism will end, and pro-Semitism will begin because they are genuine witnesses for God. In our day neither Israel nor the church is fulfilling what God intended—although I believe we are following God's program, and it is working out as He said it would. He warned us that the day would come when we would have a form of godliness but deny the power thereof.

DELIGHTS OF THE MILLENNIUM

I will greatly rejoice in the LORD, my soul shall be joyful in my God; for he hath clothed me with the garments of salvation, he hath covered me with the robe of righteousness, as a bridegroom decketh himself with ornaments, and as a bride adorneth herself with her jewels [Isa. 61:10].

"I will greatly rejoice in the LORD, my soul shall be joyful in my God"—my, they're going to have fun then! I wish that in our day more Christians had fun going to church. I wish they enjoyed it more. I wish the study of the Bible was a thrilling and exciting experience for all of us. It ought to be, and God intended that it should be.

"For he hath clothed me with the garments of salvation, he hath covered me with the robe of righteousness, as a bridegroom decketh himself with ornaments, and as a bride adorneth herself with her jewels." The Messiah continues to speak here, and as He does, all who are His can join in the psalm of praise. They will greatly rejoice in the Lord. The problem in our day is that a great many Christians can't rejoice in the Lord because they are out of fellowship. They have sin in their lives, they are way out of the will of God, and they are going on in their self-will.

For as the earth bringeth forth her bud, and as the garden causeth the things that are sown in it to spring forth; so the Lord GOD will cause righteousness and praise to spring forth before all the nations [Isa. 61:11].

Not only will there be material benefits and physical improvements, but the true blessings will be *spiritual* in that day.

CHAPTER 62

THEME: The ambition of the Messiah for Israel; the anticipation of the Millennium; announcement for that future day

The yearning of the Messiah for these anticipated joys is before us in this chapter, and there ought to be a yearning in the hearts of believers for these joys. There is a danger today of believers looking for the coming of Christ to take us out of the world so we can get away from our problems; we use it as an escape mechanism. People get into real difficulty, and then they want the Lord to come and get them out of it. When I was attending seminary, one of my fellow students was a Canadian. He was a great fellow, but he did not have much of a sense of humor, and other students, myself included, enjoyed kidding him. On certain nights after dinner he would go outside, look up into the sky, and say, "Oh, if only the Lord would come!" He would say this on the nights just before he had Hebrew class the following day. Hebrew was a difficult class, and when he said he wished the Lord would come, what he was really saying was that he wished the Lord would come because he didn't want to study Hebrew. However, at graduation time, he received his degree on one day and the next day he was married to a beautiful girl who had come down from Canada. The night before graduation this fellow went outside, looked up into the sky, and said, "I hope the Lord *doesn't* come for a few more days." Yes, that is the way it is with many of us. When things are bad, we want the Lord to come right away because we are on a hot seat and we want to get off it.

THE AMBITION OF THE MESSIAH FOR ISRAEL

For Zion's sake will I not hold my peace, and for Jerusalem's sake I will not rest, until the righteousness thereof go forth as brightness, and the salvation thereof as a lamp that burneth [Isa. 62:1].

The reason Jerusalem can't have peace today is because her Messiah is not there. He is seated at God's right hand *longing* to rule that city in righteousness. You can call it the holy city if you want to, but it is anything but holy as it is now. However, it will be holy some day and the zeal of Jehovah of Hosts will perform it. Man won't make the Kingdom, and the United Nations won't do it—that is obvious now. I don't think that anyone can bring peace into the world but this One. Only the zeal of the Lord of Hosts will accomplish it. The heart of the prophet Isaiah, as well as the heart of every godly soul on earth, enters into this longing. All of creation and all believers are groaning in their present state as they contemplate the future. Christian pilgrim, are you weary of the earthly journey, and do you desire the fellowship of the Father's house? That is a question each believer should consider.

> **And the Gentiles shall see thy righteousness, and all kings thy glory: and thou shalt be called by a new name, which the mouth of the LORD shall name [Isa. 62:2].**

A new heart, a new situation, a new earth, and a new righteousness demand a new name. I don't know what the new Vernon McGee will be like, but I'll be glad that the old Vernon McGee is gone. We will be new, and we are to be in the New Jerusalem. What a wonderful picture is given here of the future.

Redemption involves not only the church, but the nation Israel and this earth. Now we are all groaning and travailing, waiting for that grand day of deliverance.

> **Thou shalt also be a crown of glory in the hand of the LORD, and a royal diadem in the hand of thy God [Isa. 62:3].**

Israel is also going to have a new position.

> **Thou shalt no more be termed Forsaken; neither shall thy land any more be termed Desolate: but thou shalt be**

called Hephzibah, and thy land Beulah: for the Lord delighteth in thee, and thy land shall be married [Isa.
62:4].

I have heard people sing that song about "Beulah land, sweet Beulah
land," and I knew they did not have the foggiest notion what "Beulah
land" meant or where it was. Let's see what this verse is talking about.

Israel has been "Forsaken"—this is the picture and name of Israel
since the crucifixion of Christ. When you look at that land today, the
word that comes to your mind is *forsaken*—desolate. That is the description of the land right now, but in the coming Kingdom Israel
shall be called *Hephzibah*, which means "delightful." It is going to be
a delightful spot. I have made the statement before that I don't like
Jerusalem as it is today, but it will be delightful in that future day.

"And thy land Beulah"—*Beulah* means "married." In other
words, the King is present to protect it, and His presence means joy.

For as a young man marrieth a virgin, so shall thy sons
marry thee: and as the bridegroom rejoiceth over the
bride, so shall thy God rejoice over thee [Isa. 62:5].

God will delight over Israel as a bridegroom delights over a bride.

THE ANTICIPATION OF THE MILLENNIUM

I have set watchmen upon thy walls, O Jerusalem,
which shall never hold their peace day nor night: ye that
make mention of the Lord, keep not silence [Isa. 62:6].

This longing is contagious. The thirsty soul longs to drink. Every
right-thinking person can pray for the peace of Jerusalem and long for
that day when there will be peace.

And give him no rest, till he establish, and till he make
Jerusalem a praise in the earth [Isa. 62:7].

God says that He ". . . will overturn, overturn, overturn . . . until he comes whose right it is . . ." to rule (Ezek. 21:27).

ANNOUNCEMENT FOR THAT FUTURE DAY

Now let's drop down to the announcement of the Lord for that future day—

> Behold the LORD hath proclaimed unto the end of the world, Say ye to the daughter of Zion, Behold, thy salvation cometh; behold, his reward is with him, and his work before him [Isa. 62:11].

This announcement is pertinent for the present hour, as this verse indicates. The salvation of Israel is part of God's overall plan of salvation. We ought to present the gospel to every Israelite. The Messiah is their Savior today. And the second coming of Christ means the second coming of Christ to establish His Kingdom on earth for these people.

> And they shall call them, The holy people, The redeemed of the LORD: and thou shalt be called, Sought out, A city not forsaken [Isa. 62:12].

Israel cannot be called a holy people today. They are not redeemed today. Jerusalem is a forsaken city right now, but the day will come when things will be different. The experience of God's salvation will work a transformation in the nation Israel and also in the physical earth. The people will be called an holy people, and the land will be greatly desired. The contrary is true today. What a glorious future we have!

CHAPTER 63

THEME: The winepress of judgment; in wrath the Savior remembers mercy

The content of the first six verses of this chapter is certainly in contrast to the preceding section. It really seems out of keeping with the tenor of this entire section of Isaiah, but judgment precedes the Kingdom, and this has always been the divine order.

When Isaiah 53:1 described Christ at His first coming "there was no beauty that we should desire Him," but here there is majesty and beauty, which identifies this passage with His second coming. Also, the day of vengeance has been identified already with Christ's second coming rather than His first coming, as the Lord Himself clearly stated. Compare Isaiah 61:2 with Luke 44:18–20.

I find no delight in the first part of this chapter, because we see the wrath of Christ likened to a winepress in His coming judgment. Then the second part of the chapter reveals the lovingkindness which Christ manifests toward His own.

THE WINEPRESS OF JUDGMENT

Who is this that cometh from Edom, with dyed garments from Bozrah? this that is glorious in his apparel, traveling in the greatness of his strength? I that speak in righteousness, mighty to save [Isa. 63:1].

The form used here is an antiphony. Those who ask the question concerning the One coming from Edom are overwhelmed by His majesty and beauty. He comes from Edom and the east, and we are told elsewhere that His feet will touch the Mount of Olives on the east. "Edom" and "Bozrah" are geographical places, and are to be considered as such, but this does not exhaust the mind of the Spirit. Edom is symbolic of the flesh and the entire Adamic race, and here we see the judgment of man.

**Wherefore art thou red in thine apparel, and thy gar-
ments like him that treadeth in the winevat? [Isa. 63:2].**

In that day men would get into the winepress barefooted to tread out
the grapes. The red juice would spurt out of the ripe grapes and stain
their garments. That is the picture you have in this verse, and that is
why this question is asked. The spectators see that there is blood on
His beautiful garments just as if He had trodden the winepress.

Now listen to His answer—

**I have trodden the winepress alone; and of the people
there was none with me: for I will tread them in mine
anger, and trample them in my fury; and their blood
shall be sprinkled upon my garments, and I will stain
all my raiment [Isa. 63:3].**

Notice that it is *their* blood, not His.

The early church fathers associated these first six verses with the
first coming of Christ. They mistook the winepress as the suffering of
Christ on the Cross. Such an interpretation is untenable, as the blood
upon His garments is not His blood but that of others. It is the day of
vengeance. It is identified already with the second coming of Christ
rather than with His first coming. The Lord Jesus made that clear in
Luke 4:18–20 when He read Isaiah 61:2. The Lord Jesus shed His own
blood at His first coming, but that is not the picture which is presented here. He was trodden on at His first coming, but here He does
the treading. This is a frightful picture of judgment.

Now we are told the reason for His judgment—

**For the day of vengeance is in mine heart, and the year
of my redeemed is come [Isa. 63:4].**

He has come to save forever His redeemed ones from their vicious oppressors. This is His judgment upon the earth, and it is defined as the
day of vengeance.

And I looked, and there was none to help; and I wondered that there was none to uphold: therefore mine own arm brought salvation unto me; and my fury, it upheld me [Isa. 63:5].

The Lord Jesus Christ wrought salvation alone when He was on the Cross, and judgment is His solo work also.

And I will tread down the people in mine anger, and make them drunk in my fury, and I will bring down their strength to the earth [Isa. 63:6].

This is the end of man's little day upon the earth. The King is coming to the earth in judgment. There are those who will say, "This is frightful. I don't like it." Then, like the proverbial ostrich, they will put their heads in the sand and read John 14 or some other comforting passage of Scripture. However, we have to face up to this verse. The next time the Lord comes it will be in judgment. Can you think of any other way He can come and set up His Kingdom? Suppose the Lord Jesus came the second time the way he came the first time, as the Man of Galilee, the Carpenter of Nazareth who walked the countryside telling people that He had come from heaven. Suppose He knocked on the door of the Kremlin. Do you think those people are ready for Him? I don't think they are. I think they would put Him in front of a firing squad before the sun came up. No nation and no church today is prepared to turn their affairs over to Jesus. If they *are* prepared, why don't they do it? He was rejected when He came nearly two thousand years ago, and He has been rejected ever since. I can't think of any other way for Him to come the second time but in judgment.

Now others may say, "This verse is in the *Old* Testament. You have a God of wrath in the Old Testament, but when you get to the New Testament, He is a God of love." One of the reasons that the Book of Revelation has never been popular with the liberal is because it is filled with judgment. The Book of Revelation is in the *New* Testament, and the language is the strongest in the Bible (except what came from the lips of the Lord Jesus, who spoke more of hell than anyone else). The Book of Revelation speaks of Christ's coming to put down the unrighteousness and rebellion and godlessness that is on the earth. Consider this one segment of the Book of Revelation: "And I heard a great voice out of the temple saying to the seven angels, Go your ways, and pour out the vials of the wrath of God upon the earth. And the first went, and poured out his vial upon the earth; and there fell a noisome and grievous sore upon the men which had the mark of the beast, and upon them which worshipped his image. And the second angel poured out his vial upon the sea; and it became as the blood of a dead man; and every living soul died in the sea. And the third angel poured out his vial upon the rivers and fountains of waters; and they became blood. And I heard the angel of the waters say, Thou art righteous, O Lord, which art, and wast, and shall be, because thou hast judged thus" (Rev. 16:1–5). You see, immediately the critic will say, "God is not fair; He is not righteous to do this." God lets us know that when He judges like this, He is indeed being righteous. "For they have shed the blood of saints and prophets, and thou hast given them blood to drink; for they are worthy. And I heard another out of the altar say, Even so, Lord God Almighty, true and righteous are thy judgments" (Rev. 16:6–7). God is right in what He does—whether we think so or not. After all, to compare you and me with this tremendous universe would make it obvious that we don't amount to very much. Your opinion and my opinion, even when they are put together, aren't worth very much. It is what God says that is important. When God says He is righteous, but we don't think He is, that means that we are wrong. God is righteous in what He does. "And the fourth angel poured out his vial upon the sun; and power was given unto him to scorch men with fire. And men were scorched with great heat, and blasphemed the name of God, which hath power over these plagues: and they repented not to give him glory" (Rev. 16:8–9). You would think that all of this would cause them to turn to God, but they didn't react that way. Instead it just brought out what they really were—just as the plagues of Egypt did in Pharaoh's day. "And the fifth angel poured out his vial upon the seat of the beast; and his kingdom was full of darkness; and they gnawed their tongues for pain" (Rev. 16:10). I have quoted this extensive passage from the New Testament to show the agreement between the Old and New Testaments. Don't let anyone tell you that we have a God of wrath in the Old Testament and a God of love in the New Testament! The God of love is the One making these statements in both the Old and New Testaments because there is love in law—in fact, there is law in love.

Judgment is frightful, but He is coming in judgment when He returns to this earth, and He has not asked me to apologize for Him.

IN WRATH THE SAVIOR REMEMBERS MERCY

In this section we see that in wrath the Lord Jesus remembers mercy to those who are His.

> **I will mention the lovingkindnesses of the LORD, and the praises of the LORD, according to all that the LORD hath bestowed on us, and the great goodness toward the house of Israel, which he hath bestowed on them according to his mercies, and according to the multitude of his lovingkindnesses [Isa. 63:7].**

The entire content and intent changes abruptly at this point. It is like coming out of darkness into the sunlight of noonday. It is like turning from black to white. Our God is glorious in holiness, fearful in praises, doing wonders, and this is only one aspect of His many attributes. He is good, and He exhibits lovingkindness. He is also a God of mercy. If these attributes were not in evidence, we would all be consumed today—you may be sure of that! He has to come in judgment to take over this earth. It seems to me that He has given men an extra long time to turn to Him.

> **For he said, Surely they are my people, children that will not lie: so he was their Saviour [Isa. 63:8].**

His "people" here are believing Israelites and also a great company of Gentiles who will turn to Christ during the Great Tribulation. (Of course here the church has already gone to be with Him and has been in His presence for some time.)

"Children that will not lie." It sounds as if He had high hopes of them, but they disappointed Him. Certainly He expects you and me to live lives well-pleasing to Him, and He specifically admonished us, "Lie not one to another."

> **In all their affliction he was afflicted, and the angel of his presence saved them: in his love and in his pity he redeemed them; and he bare them, and carried them all the days of old [Isa. 63:9].**

How tender are these words. I believe that the angel of the Lord is none other than the pre-incarnate Christ. We are told that in His love and pity He redeemed and carried them. He entered into the sufferings of His people.

Now there has been some question about whether "in all their affliction he was afflicted" should be positive or negative. We have good manuscript evidence for the negative: "in all their affliction he was *not* afflicted." Which is true? Well, both are true, but I personally like the negative much better. Let me give you my reason. When the Lord went through the wilderness with the children of Israel, He wasn't afflicted when they were afflicted. For example, when they were bitten by the fiery serpents, He wasn't bitten. In all their affliction He was not afflicted. He was like a mother or a father who just stood by and waited for them. He didn't go on without them. The pillar of cloud and the pillar of fire were there. God was waiting for them. For forty years through that wilderness experience He was patient with them, patient like a mother.

When I was a pastor in Pasadena, my study was right by the street that led to a market. I used to watch a mother who had two children. One child she carried, and the other little fellow often walked along by himself. Sometimes the little fellow would stop, and his mother always waited for him. Sometimes when he would fall down, or stray a little, doing something he shouldn't do, she would wait patiently for

him. I often thought to myself, *That is the way God has been doing
with me all of these years.* I fall down, or I get in trouble, and God
waits for me. That is the way He does with His people.

> **But they rebelled, and vexed his holy Spirit: therefore he
> was turned to be their enemy, and he fought against
> them [Isa. 63:10].**

I think the Holy Spirit gets rather tired of you and me! But He is patient
with us. Thank God for that!

> **Then he remembered the days of old, Moses, and his
> people, saying, Where is he that brought them up out of
> the sea with the shepherd of his flock? where is he that
> put his holy spirit within him? [Isa. 63:11].**

I think this is a direct reference to Israel, but at the same time it is a
picture of the entire human family. Some expositors do not feel that
the reference here is to the Holy Spirit, the third Person of the Godhead, because the Old Testament does not contain a clear-cut distinction of the Holy Spirit. However, I believe that the Holy Spirit
mentioned here is the Holy Spirit that today dwells in believers. Although in the Old Testament we do not have a clear-cut distinction of
the work of the Holy Spirit, I believe this is definitely a mention of it.
    The Holy Spirit is the One—

> **That led them by the right hand of Moses with his glori-
> ous arm, dividing the water before them, to make him-
> self an everlasting name?**
>
> **That led them through the deep, as an horse in the wil-
> derness, that they should not stumble? [Isa. 63:12–13].**

Once again God refers to the history of their deliverance out of Egypt.
Then He continues the history of how He has led them.

Here the prophet and the people plead with God to look upon their great need and desire.

> **Look down from heaven, and behold from the habitation of thy holiness and of thy glory: where is thy zeal and thy strength, the sounding of thy bowels and of thy mercies toward me? are they restrained?**

> **Doubtless thou art our father, though Abraham be ignorant of us, and Israel acknowledge us not: thou, O LORD, art our father, our redeemer; thy name is from everlasting [Isa. 63:15–16].**

God was the *Father* of the nation Israel, but there is no thought in the Old Testament that He was the Father of the individual Israelite. It is a corporate term rather than a personal one in the Old Testament. In the New Testament it becomes personal, not corporate. As Abraham was the father of the nation and not of each individual Israelite, so God, too, was the Father of the nation.

> **O LORD, why hast thou made us to err from thy ways, and hardened our heart from thy fear? Return for thy servants' sake, the tribes of thine inheritance [Isa. 63:17].**

This is a pleading prayer, asking God to intervene for them.

> **We are thine: thou never barest rule over them; they were not called by thy name [Isa. 63:19].**

Now they surrender completely to God. This should be the attitude of the Christian today—complete yielding to God. Most of us are afraid to yield to God because we are afraid He will be hard on us. God wants to be gentle with us if we will give Him a chance. But remember that He also is the God of judgment. He is the One who is coming to earth some day to tread the winepress of the fierceness of His wrath.

God is not trying to frighten you; He is just telling you the truth.

CHAPTER 64

THEME: God's control of the universe recognized;
man's condition in the universe confessed

This chapter continues the pleading of the hungry hearts for the
presence of God in life's affairs. No child of God today can be
immune to such ardent petitions. The Christian can cry with the same
passionate desire, "Even so, come, Lord Jesus!" (see Rev. 22:20).

This, too, is a neglected section of the Word of God. We have attempted to emphasize this section so that you can see why we hold the
premillennial viewpoint and why we believe Christ is coming before
the Great Tribulation period. The church will be taken out of the
world before the Tribulation. The Lord will come at the end of the
Tribulation to establish His Kingdom. This is not just a theory. This is
what we find in the Book of Isaiah. We have looked at Isaiah almost
verse by verse, and the prophet has presented a very definite program.
The Word of God simply does not give isolated verses to prove some
particular theory of interpretation, but whatever your or my theory is,
it has to fit in place. Some of the theories I hear today remind me of the
lady who went into the shoestore to get a pair of shoes. The salesman
asked, "What size do you wear?" The lady replied that she could wear
a size four, but a size five felt so much better that she always bought a
size six or sometimes a seven. There are some theories, as far as the
Word of God is concerned, that require a size change because they
simply don't fit.

GOD'S CONTROL OF THE UNIVERSE RECOGNIZED

**Oh that thou wouldest rend the heavens, that thou
wouldest come down, that the mountains might flow
down at thy presence [Isa. 64:1].**

The prophet is a representative of the believing remnant of Israel in
that future day. Again he is using the past tense, which is called a

prophetic tense. That is, God sees it as having already taken place, and He gives the prophecy to Isaiah from the other side, looking back at the event.

The prophet is pleading with God just as the remnant of Israel will do in that day of the Great Tribulation. This Scripture is not written to us—the church is not in view here. It is addressed to the remnant of Israel, but as believers we can identify with them. Our prayer today should be for the return of the Lord. "Even so, come, Lord Jesus." But it is clear in this section that Isaiah is predicting Israel's prayer during the Great Tribulation period.

> **As when the melting fire burneth, the fire causeth the waters to boil, to make thy name known to thine adversaries, that the nations may tremble at thy presence! [Isa. 64:2].**

Just as fire makes water boil, so the presence of God would make the nations tremble. Today the nations are not conscious of the existence of God. There are people who wonder how we can sit down with godless nations like Russia or China. The reason is that we are just about as godless as they are. In our day the nations of the world are not turning to God, nor do they recognize Him. However, as the end of the age approaches, I believe there will be a very real consciousness that God is getting ready to break through. There was that consciousness throughout the world at the time of the birth of Christ, and several Roman historians have called attention to that fact.

> **When thou didst terrible things which we looked not for, thou camest down, the mountains flowed down at thy presence [Isa. 64:3].**

The very mountains melt—that is, become molten—at His presence. The enemies then will cry for the mountains to hide them from ". . . the wrath of the Lamb" (Rev. 6:16).

For since the beginning of the world men have not heard, nor perceived by ear, neither hath the eye seen, O God, beside thee, what he hath prepared for him that waiteth for him [Isa. 64:4].

Paul expresses this same thought in 1 Corinthians 2:9 when he says, "But as it is written, Eye hath not seen, nor ear heard, neither have entered into the heart of man, the things which God hath prepared for them that love him." Paul goes on to say, "But God hath revealed them unto us by his Spirit: for the Spirit searcheth all things, yea, the deep things of God" (1 Cor. 2:10). First Corinthians 2:9 is obviously a quote from Isaiah, but verse 10 tells us that in our day the Holy Spirit will reveal these things unto us. In the day of the Great Tribulation they will have to wait until Christ comes. And even for us it can be said, "For now we see through a glass, darkly; but then face to face: now I know in part; but then shall I know even as also I am known" (1 Cor. 13:12).

All through this section we can identify with these people, for we have a hope also. We are looking for Him to take us *out* of the world, and they will be looking for Him to come and establish a kingdom here on the earth.

My friend, it seems to me that the only folk who miss this distinction are the theologians. Failure to recognize that Christ is going to take the church up to meet Him in the air and that He is coming *down* to the earth to establish His Kingdom gives us some upside-down theology.

Thou meetest him that rejoiceth and worketh righteousness, those that remember thee in thy ways: behold, thou art wroth; for we have sinned: in those is continuance, and we shall be saved [Isa. 64:5].

Here begins the acknowledgment of sins and, at the same time, an expression of confidence in the redemption of the Savior.

MAN'S CONDITION IN THE UNIVERSE CONFESSED

But we are all as an unclean thing, and all our righteousnesses are as filthy rags; and we all do fade as a leaf; and our iniquities, like the wind, have taken us away [Isa. 64:6].

This verse is familiar because it is used very frequently to establish the fact that man has no righteousness *per se;* that is, man has no righteousness in himself whatsoever. This is not only true of Israel but it is also true of the entire human family. Both Jew and Gentile alike have sinned and come short of the glory of God. "We are all as an unclean thing, and all our righteousnesses are as filthy rags." It does not matter what we might consider to be good works. It may sound pretty good to give a million dollars to feed the poor and hungry or to care for little orphans and widows, but in God's sight anything that the flesh produces is as filthy rags. You cannot bring a clean thing out of an unclean thing. A lost sinner is unable to do anything that is acceptable to God—he must first come to God *His* way. This is very difficult for man to accept—especially the unsaved man who is depending upon his good works to save him.

But now, O LORD, thou art our father; we are the clay, and thou our potter; and we all are the work of thy hand [Isa. 64:8].

God is our Father by creation, but man lost that image. You and I can become sons of God in only one way, and that is through Christ. The New Testament revelation of the sons of God is not by creation at all, but on an entirely different basis. In John 1:12–13 we read, "But as many as received him, to them gave he power to become the sons of God, even to them that believe on his name: Which were born, not of blood, nor of the will of the flesh, nor of the will of man, but of God."

"We all are the work of thy hand" is a recognition that God is our Creator. He is the Potter, the One who creates. Now, a man that makes a vessel or a pretty vase is, in a sense, the father of it. In this same way we speak of George Washington as being the father of our country.

Paul makes this distinction in his speech in Athens: "For in him we live, and move, and have our being; as certain also of your own poets have said, For we are also his offspring. Forasmuch then as we are the offspring of God, we ought not to think that the Godhead is like unto gold, or silver, or stone, graven by art and man's device" (Acts 17:28–29). Man is the *offspring* of God in that he was created by Him, but not all men are the born-again *sons* of God. Paul is saying that since God has created us, we ought not to make an image and say that it is a likeness of God. In doing so we would be attempting to create God, and God has forbidden that.

> **Thy holy cities are a wilderness, Zion is a wilderness, Jerusalem a desolation [Isa. 64:10].**

The description given in this verse was not true in Isaiah's day, but it came to pass shortly afterwards when Babylon came against Jerusalem. Second Kings 25:9–10 tell us, "And he burnt the house of the LORD, and the king's house, and all the houses of Jerusalem, and every great man's house burnt he with fire. And all the army of the Chaldees, that were with the captain of the guard, brake down the walls of Jerusalem round about." Isaiah's prophecy was literally fulfilled.

> **Our holy and our beautiful house, where our fathers praised thee, is burned up with fire: and all our pleasant things are laid waste [Isa. 64:11].**

Isaiah writes as if this has already taken place, but it didn't happen until about one hundred years after Isaiah. The temple was destroyed at the same time Jerusalem was destroyed.

> **Wilt thou refrain thyself for these things, O LORD? wilt thou hold thy peace, and afflict us very sore? [Isa. 64:12].**

The prophet closes this chapter with a question: Will God refuse to act? The remainder of Isaiah's prophecy is God's answer to this question. God rejected Israel only after they rejected Him, but it did not thwart His plan and purpose for them and for the earth. God has carried through with His program, which is yet to be finalized.

CHAPTER 65

THEME: Redeemer's reason for rejecting the nation; reservation of a remnant; revelation of the new heavens and the new earth

In chapter 64 we noted the ferevent prayer of the prophet and the people pleading with the King to break through all barriers and come to earth. Chapters 65 and 66 contain God's answer to that plea. God makes it very clear that their sins and unfaithfulness are responsible for His judgment upon them, but that their sins have not frustrated His promises and purposes concerning the coming Kingdom. God has preserved a remnant through which He will fulfill all of His prophecies. Again He gives a vision of the Kingdom and a prospectus of the eternal position of Israel in the new heavens and new earth. This will take us to the end of the Book of Isaiah which goes down in a blaze of glory.

REDEEMER'S REASON FOR REJECTING THE NATION

I am sought of them that asked not for me; I am found of them that sought me not: I said, Behold me, behold me, unto a nation that was not called by my name [Isa. 65:1].

He is speaking here of the Gentiles to whom the gospel has now come. When Paul came to Philippi he had had the vision of the man in Macedonia. However, when he got over there, he found, not a *man* looking for him wanting to hear the gospel, but a *woman* by the name of Lydia who was holding a prayer meeting down by the river. Although she may not have recognized her need, Paul brought the gospel to her.

Paul quotes this verse in Romans 10:20: "But Esaias is very bold, and saith, I was found of them that sought me not; I was made manifest unto them that asked not after me." That is the way it happened to us, my friend. Our ancestors were heathen barbarians. They were not down on the shore with their hands held out, saying, "Oh please, send us missionaries!" They didn't want them; they even killed some of those who did come. Today the heathen are not begging for the gospel—nobody's begging for the gospel. God has responded to people who didn't even call upon Him. I never asked to be saved—He just saved me. I was like the black boy down south who said, "I ran from Him as fast as my sinful legs would carry me and as far as my rebellious heart would take me, and He took out after me and ran me down." That is the way it happened for all of us who have been saved.

I have spread out my hands all the day unto a rebellious people, which walketh in a way that was not good, after their own thoughts [Isa. 65:2].

Now He is talking to the Jew, to the nation Israel. God first gave the gospel to him; it was given "to the Jew first." Again, in Romans 10:21, Paul says, "But to Israel he saith, All day long have I stretched forth my hands unto a disobedient and gainsaying people." God rejected them only after they rejected Him. In Acts 13:46 we read: "Then Paul and Barnabas waxed bold, and said, It was necessary that the word of God should first have been spoken to you: but seeing ye put it from you, and judge yourselves unworthy of everlasting life, lo, we turn to the Gentiles." That is the way it all came about. In other words, if Jerusalem refuses the gospel, Ephesus will receive it. If Los Angeles rejects the gospel, then maybe Bombay, India, or some out-of-the-way place is going to hear. The flood tide of God's grace *will* spill over somewhere in this world. Thank God for that.

A people that provoketh me to anger continually to my face; that sacrificeth in gardens, and burneth incense upon altars of brick [Isa. 65:3].

This is the reason that blessings were withheld from Israel: they were continually going into idolatry and rebelling against God.

>Which remain among the graves, and lodge in the monuments, which eat swine's flesh, and broth of abominable things is in their vessels;

>Which say, Stand by thyself, come not near to me; for I am holier than thou. These are a smoke in my nose, a fire that burneth all the day [Isa. 65:4–5].

This is just a partial list of the reasons for Israel's rejection. They were breaking the commandments God gave to them.

>Behold, it is written before me: I will not keep silence, but will recompense, even recompense into their bosom.

>Your iniquities, and the iniquities of your fathers together, saith the Lord, which have burned incense upon the mountains, and blasphemed me upon the hills: therefore will I measure their former work into their bosom [Isa. 65:6–7].

Israel walked in pride. They practiced the eternalities of a God-given religion, but their hearts were far from God. They practiced iniquity as easily as they practiced the rituals of religion. In so doing, they blasphemed God.

RESERVATION OF A REMNANT

A remnant is reserved through which all of God's promises are to be fulfilled. God always has had a remnant.

>Thus saith the Lord, As the new wine is found in the cluster, and one saith, Destroy it not; for a blessing is in it; so will I do for my servants' sakes, that I may not destroy them all [Isa. 65:8].

In spite of their sins, God would not totally exterminate them because of the believing remnant. The remnant is compared to a cluster of wonderful grapes that has been passed over in the vineyard.

> And I will bring forth a seed out of Jacob, and out of
> Judah an inheritor of my mountains: and mine elect
> shall inherit it, and my servants shall dwell there [Isa.
> 65:9].

"A seed out of Jacob" could refer to the Lord Jesus Christ, and in one
sense I think it does, but more particularly it refers to the remnant out
of Israel that is to be saved. For the sake of the remnant God will make
good His promises.

> And Sharon shall be a fold of flocks, and the valley of
> Achor a place for the herds to lie down in, for my people
> that have sought me [Isa. 65:10].

You see, there was to be a place, a place of safety for the little flock, for
the remnant.

> But ye are they that forsake the LORD, that forget my holy
> mountain, that prepare a table for that troop, and that
> furnish the drink offering unto that number.

> Therefore will I number you to the sword, and ye shall
> all bow down to the slaughter: because when I called, ye
> did not answer; when I spake, ye did not hear; but did
> evil before mine eyes, and did choose that wherein I de-
> lighted not [Isa. 65:11–12].

But for the remainder of the nation that went headlong without heed-
ing the Word of God, there remains nothing but punishment. I do not
understand how intelligent people who believe in the existence of
God can fail to realize that there must finally come a judgment and a
straightening out of things. If they continue on in sin, they will be
judged, as surely as God judged the bulk of the nation Israel.

> Behold, my servants shall sing for joy of heart, but ye
> shall cry for sorrow of heart, and shall howl for vexation
> of spirit [Isa. 65:14].

Just as God made a distinction between the nation as a whole and the remnant, he makes the same distinction in the contemporary church. The church is a vast organization with a tremendously bloated membership. The question is asked as to whether the church will go through the Great Tribulation period. Well, there is a church that will go through the Great Tribulation. It is called an old harlot in Revelation 17. It is just an organization and does not belong to Christ. It is not His bride at all. The true believers in the body of Christ will be taken out before the Great Tribulation period. We need to recognize that there is a distinction to be made between that which is merely outward and that which is genuine.

REVELATION OF THE NEW HEAVENS AND THE NEW EARTH

For, behold, I create new heavens and a new earth: and the former shall not be remembered, nor come into mind [Isa. 65:17].

Here the creation of the new heavens and the new earth seems to precede chronologically the setting up of the Kingdom. But I think when we examine it closely we find that the remnant has already judged the Kingdom. The others have been judged and do not enter the Kingdom. The Lord Jesus made this clear in Matthew 25:34 when He said, ". . . Come, ye blessed of my Father, inherit the kingdom prepared for you from the foundation of the world." The others were to be cast into outer darkness and would not enter the Kingdom.

Now at the end of the millennial Kingdom—that is, at the end of the thousand-year reign of Christ, after that final rebellion—the creation of the new heavens and new earth takes place. You see, after the Rapture and during the Millennium tremendous changes in the earth will be made. The desert is going to blossom as the rose. But when you get to the new heavens and the new earth, there will not be any sea and there actually will not be any desert. It will be a *new* earth. We will have traded in the old model and gotten a new one.

I deal with this subject further in a little book I have called *Three*

Worlds in One. The message comes from 2 Peter 3 where we find that there are three worlds. There is the world that was—that which was destroyed by the waters of the Noahic flood. Then there is the present world, which is going to be destroyed by fire. And finally there will come into existence the new heavens and the new earth.

> **But be ye glad and rejoice for ever in that which I create: for, behold, I create Jerusalem a rejoicing, and her people a joy [Isa. 65:18].**

Here Isaiah is definitely speaking of the millennial blessings as well as the eternal blessings. The millennial Kingdom is a phase of the eternal Kingdom, but it is also a time of judgment. I do not think you can bring in a new heaven and a new earth until God's program of judgment is completed. When judgment is over, then we are ready for all things to be made new. I believe that after the Millennium there is something even more wonderful in store for the child of God. Man's potential will be greatly increased. Jerusalem will be a city of joy. It is not that today. It has a Wailing Wall and very few smiling people. But the day will come when God will make it a city of joy.

> **And I will rejoice in Jerusalem, and joy in my people: and the voice of weeping shall be no more heard in her, nor the voice of crying [Isa. 65:19].**

What a change there is going to be for Jerusalem!

> **There shall be no more thence an infant of days, nor an old man that hath not filled his days: for the child shall die an hundred years old; but the sinner being an hundred years old shall be accursed [Isa. 65:20].**

The longevity of life that predated the patriarchs will be one of the features of the Kingdom. People will live a long time. There won't be any need for senior citizen homes because there won't be any senior citizens. All of us will be young!

And they shall build houses, and inhabit them; and they shall plant vineyards, and eat the fruit of them [Isa. 65:21].

Prosperity is another feature of the Kingdom. It will be a time of real blessing.

They shall not build, and another inhabit; they shall not plant, and another eat: for as the days of a tree are the days of my people, and mine elect shall long enjoy the work of their hands [Isa. 65:22].

There will be permanence and stability.

The wolf and the lamb shall feed together, and the lion shall eat straw like the bullock: and dust shall be the serpent's meat. They shall not hurt nor destroy in all my holy mountain, saith the LORD [Isa. 65:25].

This is not what happens today, my friend. If the wolf and the lamb lie down together, it is the wolf feeding on the lamb. A wolf likes lamb chops. But in that day they will be together, and the lion will eat straw. I like to tell the story of the young upstart who publicly questioned Dr. George Gill in a meeting, saying, "Who ever heard of a lion eating straw? Anyone knows that a lion never eats straw!" Dr. Gill, in his characteristically easygoing manner, said, "Young man, if you can make a lion, then I will make him eat straw. The One who created the lion will equip him to eat straw when He wants him to do it." In other words, in that day the sharp fang and the bloody claw will no longer rule animal life. The law of the jungle will be changed to conform to the rule of the King. There will be nothing to hurt or harm or make afraid in the whole world. It will be a *new* world then, will it not?

CHAPTER 66

THEME: *The Creator, Ruler, Redeemer, Judge, Regenerator, and Rewarder; the Lord decides the destiny of both the saved and the lost*

Today our prayer is, "Thy kingdom come . . ." (Matt. 6:10). In Isaiah 66 the Kingdom has come.

THE CREATOR, RULER, REDEEMER, JUDGE, REGENERATOR, AND REWARDER

Thus saith the Lord, The heaven is my throne, and the earth is my footstool: where is the house that ye build unto me? and where is the place of my rest? [Isa. 66:1].

"The earth is my footstool"—this little earth on which you and I live is not very important. It is only a footstool for God!

"Where is the house that ye build unto me? and where is the place of my rest?" Any temple down here on this earth could not contain Him. Solomon recognized that. In his prayer of dedication for the first temple, he said, "But will God indeed dwell on the earth? behold, the heaven and heaven of heavens cannot contain thee; how much less this house that I have builded?" (1 Kings 8:27). Therefore, the eternal character of the Kingdom seems to me to be the very presence of God. You won't need a temple there. I think that the New Jerusalem (Rev. 21) will be a place to which the people on earth will come to worship and visit.

Listen to the God of creation, the God who is high and holy and lifted up:

For all those things hath mine hand made, and all those things have been, saith the Lord: but to this man will I

> look, even to him that is poor and of a contrite spirit,
> and trembleth at my word [Isa. 66:2].

The God who created this vast universe, who is above it and beyond it, condescends to dwell with the humble and contrite of heart. Oh, what condescension on the part of God! In that day the meek shall inherit the earth; in fact, they will inherit all things.

> He that killeth an ox is as if he slew a man; he that sacri-
> ficeth a lamb, as if he cut off a dog's neck; he that of-
> fereth an oblation, as if he offered swine's blood; he that
> burneth incense, as if he blessed an idol. Yea, they have
> chosen their own ways, and their soul delighteth in
> their abominations [Isa. 66:3].

Apparently the sacrificial system will be dispensed with after the Millennium. To offer an ox without spiritual comprehension is the same as murder. Everything in eternity must point to Christ—or that which was once commanded becomes sin.

> Hear the word of the LORD, ye that tremble at his word;
> Your brethren that hated you, that cast you out for my
> name's sake, said, Let the LORD be glorified: but he shall
> appear to your joy, and they shall be ashamed [Isa.
> 66:5].

God will make the distinction between the true and the false—that which is real and that which is not. Christ said to let the wheat and tares grow together, that He would separate them. Now that time has come. The Pharisee who was meticulous in his religious practice is to be cast out. The publican who stood afar off and repented will be received.

> A voice of noise from the city, a voice from the temple, a
> voice of the LORD that rendereth recompence to his ene-
> mies [Isa. 66:6].

God will finally deal with the enemies of Israel—they are *His* enemies also.

> **Before she travailed, she brought forth; before her pain came, she was delivered of a man child [Isa. 66:7].**

The Great Tribulation will be a time of travail. Israel will go through the Great Tribulation *after* Christ is born in Bethlehem—"before her pain came, she was delivered of a man child" who is Christ Jesus. This is a remarkable verse.

> **Shall I bring to the birth, and not cause to bring forth? saith the LORD: shall I cause to bring forth, and shut the womb? saith thy God [Isa. 66:9].**

God will make sure that all He has promised is accomplished. The 144,000 Jews who are sealed at the beginning of the Great Tribulation will come through it—not just 143,999, but everyone of them will be there. How wonderful!

Now he can say:

> **Rejoice with Jerusalem, and be glad with her, all ye that love her: rejoice for joy with her, all ye that mourn for her [Isa. 66:10].**

What a time of blessing it will be.

THE LORD DECIDES THE DESTINY OF BOTH THE SAVED AND THE LOST

> **For I know their works and their thoughts: it shall come, that I will gather all nations and tongues; and they shall come, and see my glory [Isa. 66:18].**

All nations must appear before Him. The Lord Jesus mentioned this in Matthew 25:31–32. "When the Son of man shall come in his glory, and all the holy angels with him, then shall he sit upon the throne of his glory: And before him shall be gathered all nations: and he shall separate them one from another as a shepherd divideth his sheep from the goats." At that time a great company of Gentiles are going to be saved as well as many from Israel. The nations are going to come and worship in Jerusalem.

> **For as the new heavens and the new earth, which I will make, shall remain before me, saith the LORD, so shall your seed and your name remain [Isa. 66:22].**

God's purposes and promises for Israel are as eternal as the new heavens and the new earth.

> **And it shall come to pass, that from one new moon to another, and from one sabbath to another, shall all flesh come to worship before me, saith the LORD [Isa. 66:23].**

The redeemed of all ages will worship God throughout eternity. That will be the most engaging and important business of eternity.

> **And they shall go forth, and look upon the carcases of the men that have transgressed against me: for their worm shall not die, neither shall their fire be quenched; and they shall be an abhorring unto all flesh [Isa. 66:24].**

In other words, "There is no peace, saith my God, to the wicked" (Isa. 57:21). That is going to be their condition throughout eternity—no peace, no rest, no contentment, no God. The Book of Isaiah closes with this third warning that there is no peace for the wicked. "He that hath ears to hear, let him hear" (Matt. 11:15).

BIBLIOGRAPHY
(Recommended for Further Study)

Criswell, W. A. *Isaiah*. Grand Rapids, Michigan: Zondervan Publishing House, 1977.

Gaebelein, Arno C. *The Annotated Bible*. Neptune, New Jersey: Loizeaux Brothers, 1917.

Ironside, H. A. *Expository Notes on Isaiah*. Neptune, New Jersey: Loizeaux Brothers, 1952.

Jennings, F. C. *Studies in Isaiah*. Neptune, New Jersey: Loizeaux Brothers, n.d.

Jensen, Irving L. *Isaiah and Jeremiah*. Chicago, Illinois: Moody Press. (A self-study guide.)

Kelly, William. *An Exposition of Isaiah*. Addison, Illinois: Bible Truth Publishers, 1896.

Martin, Alfred. *Isaiah: The Salvation of Jehovah*. Chicago, Illinois: Moody Press, 1956. (A fine, inexpensive survey.)

Martin, Alfred and John A. *Isaiah*. Chicago, Illinois: Moody Press, 1983.

McGee, J. Vernon. *Initiation Into Isaiah*. 2 vols. Pasadena, California: Thru the Bible Books, 1957.

Unger, Merrill F. *Unger's Bible Handbook*. Chicago, Illinois: Moody Press, 1966.

Unger, Merrill F. *Unger's Commentary on the Old Testament*. Chicago, Illinois: Moody Press, 1982. (Highly recommended.)

Vine, W. E. *Isaiah*. Grand Rapids, Michigan: Zondervan Publishing House, 1946.